INTEGRITY

A study on the life of Joseph

פֵּסׄור
(Joseph's Hebrew name)

© 2015 by TGS International, a wholly owned subsidiary of Christian Aid Ministries, Berlin, Ohio.

All rights reserved. No part of this book may be used, reproduced, or stored in any retrieval system, in any form or by any means, electronic or mechanical, without written permission from the publisher except for brief quotations embodied in critical articles and reviews.

All Scripture quotations are taken from the King James Version (KJV).

ISBN: 978-1-941213-63-6

Cover design and layout: Teresa Sommers
Cover graphic: © Windowseat - Fotolia
Maps by Gavin Miles

Printed in China.

Second printing: December 2016

Published by:
TGS International
P.O. Box 355
Berlin, Ohio 44610 USA
Phone: 330-893-4828
Fax: 330-893-2305
www.tgsinternational.com

TGS0001365

TAKE THE BIBLE FOR REAL

 ## IT'S UP-TO-DATE

Today, the Bible is often tragically disregarded and labeled as quaint tradition or outdated myth. It is considered unscientific and unprovable, detached from the real world, irrelevant and pointless.

I believe we need a fresh respect for the Scriptures. I want us to recapture an excitement and awe for the Bible. We must see it as historically accurate, scientifically correct, and essential to life. As we analyze the Bible, we will find that it stands up under scrutiny and welcomes proving. As we study its teachings and obey its guidance, we will find it highly relevant for the problems of today.

 ## IT'S WHAT GOD WANTS US TO KNOW

The Bible is not just another book. It is the very Word of God—perfect and practical, accurate and realistic. Without apology, God tells us how to live and brings His Word into our own experience. The Bible has all the answers for life (2 Peter 1:3). It is pertinent to the issues of every generation and speaks to all cultures, social classes, genders, and age groups.

IT'S A PROGRESSIVE UNVEILING OF WHO GOD IS

The whole Bible is about redemption, revealing Jesus Christ, the God-man, as our Redeemer. The accounts given in the Bible are not a series of unrelated stories, but God's progressive revelation of Himself, showing His character, His love, and His desire to save mankind. The stories of the Old Testament are but pieces of the whole story—His Story. My hope is that this Bible study course will give you a foundation for understanding God, His plan throughout history, and His claim on our lives.

 ## IT'S FULL OF LESSONS FROM OTHERS

In studying Bible characters, we will learn how to live in God's will. The characters are in touch with reality—with the common struggles of humanity. We will see both godly and ungodly examples. The Bible does not gloss over the faults of its characters, but shows them to be human. The inclusion of sinners in the Bible is not meant to excuse our sin; rather, their stories are included as warnings and examples of God's grace and forgiveness.

 ## IT'S INSPIRED

The Bible is the inspired Word of God. Although God used human writers, the ultimate author is God Himself. It is God-breathed. It will speak to you if you listen. It will change you if you let it. It is a message from God to you.

—*Jon Kropf*

THE LIFE OF JOSEPH

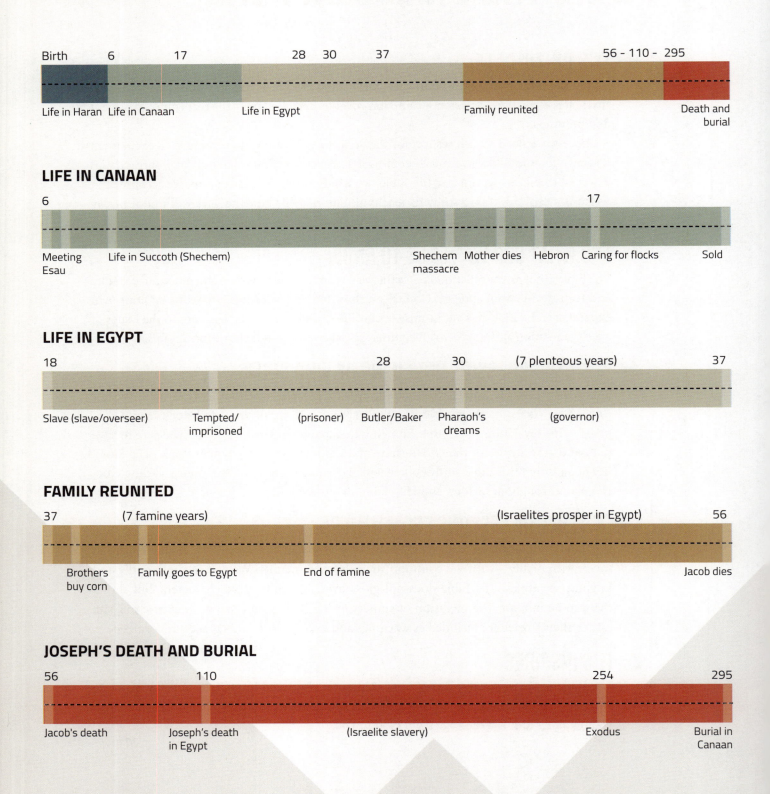

INTEGRITY

**Having high moral character; honesty;
To be complete, solid, without blemish.**

God included the story of Joseph in the Bible not to entertain us, but to give us an example. Joseph faced struggles and temptations that are common to our lives. His responses to these trials teach us lessons for today. His life is encapsulated in the word *integrity*. Joseph was honest, pure, and noble in spite of incredible odds.

HOW TO USE THIS BOOK

This book is divided into two parts. The first part is the Workbook. The second is the Lesson Background Material. The lesson background material expounds on the life of Joseph and explores what his feelings may have been. It also provides additional information, illustrations, and discussion helps. It is useful for teacher's preparation or for students to work through on their own.

The lesson background material does not need to be read *during* class time. Individuals may enjoy reading it on their own before or after the lesson. Teachers may briefly give a description of the lesson highlights, outline the parts of Joseph's life that illustrate or emphasize that day's particular lesson, and spend time looking up Bible verses. The bulk of a class period can be spent on discussion questions and activities designed to make the lessons practical to life.

Reading Scripture texts together is valuable. Don't skip over the Bible passages. This study is designed to be used with the KJV.

This book can be used as ten individual lessons in vacation Bible school, in small group studies, or in personal Bible study. These lessons may also be used as a Bible curriculum for homeschooling families. Each lesson is divided into five sections and may be done as a weekly lesson (one section for each day). A short quiz follows each lesson to test what you have learned. The sections are labeled as follows:

Analyzing God's Word

Building Your Word Knowledge

Comparing Scripture with Scripture

Discussing and Pondering

Engaging Yourself—Memorization and Application

The first section, Analyzing God's Word, is the foundation for each lesson and actually gets you into the study of Joseph's life. The following sections expand the theme of that particular lesson, tie it to the rest of Scripture, and make it practical to our lives.

Several activities in this study require a *Strong's Concordance* and an English dictionary. A topical Bible and a cross-reference aid are also beneficial.

NOTE: A separate answer key booklet is available from the publisher. It includes suggested answers for those exercises in which the answers may vary.

TABLE OF CONTENTS

TAKE THE BIBLE FOR REAL III
TIMELINE OF JOSEPH'S LIFE IV
HOW TO USE THIS BOOK VI

PART ONE: The Workbook 9
    1. Family Influences 10
    2. Trials and Disappointments 18
    3. Respect, Honor, and Obedience 28
    4. Moral Purity 36
    5. Samson: A Life of Dishonor 48
    6. Success and Responsibility 60
    7. Preparing for Famine 70
    8. Joseph Tests His Brothers 80
    9. Revenge or Forgiveness? 92
    10. Jesus—Deliverer for Mankind 102

PART TWO: Lesson Background Material 113
    1. Family Influences 114
    2. Trials and Disappointments 120
    3. Respect, Honor, and Obedience 124
    4. Moral Purity 128
    5. Samson: A Life of Dishonor 132
    6. Success and Responsibility 134
    7. Preparing for Famine 138
    8. Joseph Tests His Brothers 142
    9. Revenge or Forgiveness? 146
    10. Jesus—Deliverer for Mankind 150
        Maps 154

‹ part one ›
WORKBOOK

LESSON 1

Family Influences

"For the eyes of the LORD run to and fro throughout the whole earth, to shew himself strong in the behalf of them whose heart is perfect toward him" (2 Chronicles 16:9).

Amid the greed, idolatry, jealousy, and hatred of Joseph's world, the prospects looked dark for finding a man who was pure, sincere, and moldable in the hands of God. This is what makes Joseph's noble integrity so outstanding. Joseph grew up among dishonorable people—even his own family was ungodly in many ways—and his life is highlighted by the low character of those around him. Joseph chose the high road. Although Joseph experienced rejection and cruelty, he chose to allow these experiences to make him *better*, not *bitter*.

Many people believe the lie that they cannot control their conduct because of their upbringing, their environment, or the abuse they have experienced. But Joseph's example shows us that we cannot blame poor choices on victimization. A dysfunctional home life or mistreatment by others is not an excuse for uncontrolled passions.

www.padfield.com

We may be influenced by others, but we must take responsibility for our own actions.

In this lesson, we will consider the life of Joseph's father, mother, and brothers to see how their influence shaped Joseph's character. Favoritism and jealousy thrust Joseph into the midst of a family feud, but in spite of Joseph's difficulties at home, he chose to be different from his family and to walk in integrity. Through the power of God, we can do the same.

EXERCISES

‹ Analyzing God's Word ›

Write your thoughts.

1. Genesis 25:29–34; 27:15–36; 30:40–43; 32:6–8, 13, 24–26; 33:18–20
   How would you describe Joseph's father, Jacob? What did he pursue? How did he deceive others? What sort of bargains did he make?

2. Genesis 29:20–32; 30:1–4; 31:17–35
   What character did Joseph's mother, Rachel, display? What hurts did she have? What competition did she face within the family? Do you think there was peace in this home?

3. Genesis 34:1–7, 13–17, 24–25; 49:5–7
   What was the spirit of Joseph's brothers, especially Simeon and Levi? What did they do?

4. Genesis 35:22; 49:3–4; 1 Chronicles 5:1–2
   What character fault did Reuben have?

5. Genesis 37:2–35
   What was the attitude of Joseph's brothers toward him? Why was Joseph his father's favorite?

‹ Building Your Word Knowledge ›

Match the words to their definitions. A dictionary may be useful.

1. .... Character
2. .... Choice
3. .... Responsibility
4. .... Reputation
5. .... Victim
6. .... Environment
7. .... Influences
8. .... Companions
9. .... Examples

a. moral, legal, or mental accountability; being answerable for one's own conduct or obligation
b. an attribute, quality, or trait that distinguishes an individual
c. a definition of who you are based upon others' observation of your character
d. the power to freely select an outcome after consideration
e. one acted upon by force; one injured or destroyed
f. good and bad patterns or models that you may follow or imitate
g. the background, circumstances, or conditions by which you are surrounded
h. those things which have the power to affect you in indirect or unseen ways
i. comrades or associates by whom you are closely influenced

‹ Birthrights and Blessings ›

Write your thoughts.

10. What was so special about the birthright and blessing that Jacob took from his brother?

....

The Birthright

The *birthright* included:
- The "right" of the firstborn son to a double portion of the inheritance (Deuteronomy 21:17).
- Responsibility over the rest of the family. The eldest son usually became the patriarch at the death of the father. He inherited his father's rank and position as the head of the family, kingdom, or tribe, with the right to make decisions, orders, and judgments.
- Recognition as the spiritual leader of the family. The head of the family was responsible to offer sacrifices and to invoke the blessings of God on everyone in the home.
- A specific consecration to God (Exodus 22:29).
- A special benediction or blessing from the father.

Write your thoughts.

11. Genesis 25:34 says Esau despised his birthright. Which provisions of the birthright did Esau despise? Which ones do you think he wanted to have?

....

....

The Blessing

The *blessing* was:
- A pronouncement of God's blessings—divine favor and benefits—on the recipient.
- The means of passing on the promises of God's covenant.
- Included in the birthright, yet it could be given to others as well.

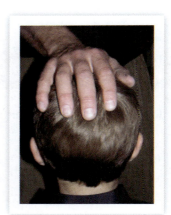

Jon Kropf

‹ The Laying On of Hands ›

In the Bible, people laid their hands on someone when they were giving a prophetic pronouncement, imparting a gift or commission, praying for healing, or giving a prayer of blessing or committal (Numbers 27:18–20; Acts 13:3; 1 Timothy 4:14; Mark 10:16; Luke 4:40).

The laying on of hands imparted worth and honor. It showed blessing or support of the recipient's life. It was given by elders, ministers, priests, or heads of households.

We need to bless those around us. It is important that we speak words of blessing, appreciation, and affirmation to others. Take time to say, "I love you!" Through a kind word or a meaningful touch, we communicate our love and value for someone and motivate them to succeed.

Look for the good in others. Express how much you value them. Who is someone you need to honor today?

"The LORD bless thee, and keep thee: the LORD make his face shine upon thee, and be gracious unto thee: the LORD lift up his countenance upon thee, and give thee peace" (Numbers 6:24–26).

‹ Comparing Scripture with Scripture ›

‹ Cross-References ›

Proverbs 22:1 says, "A good name is rather to be chosen than great riches, and loving favour rather than silver and gold." The word *name* here refers to what we might call someone's *reputation*. The Bible has much to say about our name and character.

Look up the following verses about names, reputation, and character; then see if you can find any other verses that could be linked to them.

		Observations about a name or reputation	Related verses
1.	Exodus 33:17, 19		
2.	Exodus 34:5–8		
3.	2 Samuel 7:8–9		
4.	Nehemiah 9:10		
5.	Psalm 119:63		
6.	Proverbs 28:7		
7.	Malachi 3:16		
8.	Luke 9:48		
9.	John 1:47–48		
10.	John 14:13		
11.	Philippians 2:15		
12.	Philippians 4:3		

‹ What's in a Name? ›

In Bible times, names stood for a life experience or character quality. Names showed someone's worth and gave purpose to his life. When a person had a life-changing experience, his name could be changed. God often renamed someone to signify a special plan He had for his life.

We can encourage others by giving them affirming titles. Demeaning names that poke fun can be used to humiliate or destroy someone. Proverbs tells us that life and death are in the power of the tongue. Labels show the worth you place on people.

It is interesting to note the prophetic blessings that Jacob pronounced on his sons in Genesis 49. The blessings closely match their characters and names.

Write names to match their definitions.

Abram: high father (Genesis 12:4)

13. ....: father of a multitude (Genesis 17:5)

Jacob: to take by force or deceit; to grasp the heel (Genesis 25:26; 27:36)

14. ....: prince, prevail with God (Genesis 32:28)

Leah: weary, tired (Genesis 29:17)

15. ....: shepherdess (Genesis 29:9)

16. ....: see or respect, son of vision (Genesis 29:32)

Simeon: to hear intently, son who hears/obeys (Genesis 29:33)

17. ....: attached or joined to (Genesis 29:34)

Judah: praise (Genesis 29:35)

Dan/Dinah: to judge (Genesis 30:6)

18. ....: wrestlings or struggles (Genesis 30:8)

Gad: troop (Genesis 30:11)

Asher: blessed, happy (Genesis 30:13)

19. ....: hire, recompense (Genesis 30:18)

20. ....: habitation, dwelling (Genesis 30:20)

21. ....: add or increase (Genesis 30:24)

‹ Discussing and Pondering ›

Write your thoughts.

1. Heartache comes to generations of people when we violate God's plan of marriage between one man and one woman for life. Jacob did this with polygamy. In what ways have your ancestors' family lifestyle choices blessed you or caused you grief?

   ....
   ....
   ....

2. Do you consider an inheritance of money a blessing or a curse?

   ....

3. Proverbs 11:13 says, "A talebearer revealeth secrets: but he that is of a faithful spirit concealeth the matter." Do you think it was good for Joseph to report the evil deeds of his brothers to his father? What does it mean to be a talebearer or gossip?

   ....
   ....
   ....

4. Trouble will come to our lives as it did to Joseph. Who is to blame for our sins and failures?

   ....

Fill in the blanks.

5. Romans 5:12; 3:10–11, 23 – "........................... have sinned."

6. James 1:13–16 – "He is drawn away of his ...."

7. Can we be faithful in family situations that are less than ideal? ....

8. 1 Corinthians 10:12–13 – "[God] will with the temptation also make a way to ...."

9. 1 John 2:1 – ". . . that ye .... not."

Answer *True* or *False*.

10. It is impossible to break a generational pattern of sin. ....

11. I am accountable for my sin in spite of what others have done. ....

12. I will be punished by God for the sins of my parents. ....

Answer the following questions.

13. Look at Ezekiel 18:4, 20. Do we benefit by having good parents? Will it save us?
....

‹ Engaging Yourself—Memorization and Application ›

Write your thoughts.

1. Is your connection with God only because of your parents, or can you say that He is *your* God? Are you personally acquainted with Him? Does He know you?
....
....
....

2. What are some qualities that you want to build in your life? What do you want to be known for?
....
....
....

3. Think about Joseph's family legacy. What kind of people do you hope your children and grandchildren will be?
....
....
....

4. What are some ways you can leave a legacy of blessing for your children? (Proverbs 20:7)

....

....

....

....

Memorize 2 Corinthians 4:16b–17. You may find the following activity helpful to familiarize yourself with it. Draw a line through the listed words and phrases in the puzzle. The words may run up, down, across, and diagonally.

‹ Hidden Verse ›

```
T  H  O  U  G  H  D  L  I  G  H  T  D  A
I  C  W  U  U  F  Y  A  R  L  T  B  D  F
N  I  E  W  T  B  A  A  Y  N  G  U  H  F
W  H  D  O  7  W  F  I  E  L  N  T  S  L
A  W  E  R  1  A  A  M  N  A  I  F  I  I
R  O  W  K  6  E  O  R  M  T  D  O  R  C
D  F  E  E  1  M  P  I  D  I  E  R  E  T
U  G  N  T  :  D  N  A  D  S  E  A  P  I
R  L  E  H  4  E  S  U  A  C  C  T  R  O
U  O  R  H  R  R  O  F  Y  T  X  E  O  N
O  R  E  C  O  R  U  O  X  H  E  Y  F  E
J  Y  S  I  C  T  H  G  I  E  W  O  R  R
N  O  T  H  2  E  L  A  N  R  E  T  E  O
M  K  Q  W  T  U  B  V  F  O  R  U  S  M
```

2 Cor 4:16-17						
For	not;	perish,	renewed	light	worketh	eternal
which	but	yet	day	affliction,	for us	weight
cause	though	the	by	which	a far	of glory.
we	our	inward	day.	is	more	
faint	outward	man	For	but for a	exceeding	
	man	is	our	moment,	and	

16 Integrity: A study on the life of Joseph

‹ Quiz 1 ›

Answer *True* or *False*.

1. Responsibility is being answerable for your own conduct. ....

2. An influence has absolute power over you and can force you to do something. ....

Answer the questions.

3. Why was Joseph his father's favorite son?

   ....
   ....

4. Was Joseph loved and appreciated by his brothers?

   ....

5. What did Joseph's uncle Esau despise?

   ....

6. What is "rather to be chosen than great riches"?

   ....

7. Whose name meant "deceit"?

   ....

8. Whose name meant "to add or increase"?

   ....

9. Whose sins are you accountable for?

   ....

10. Write 2 Corinthians 4:16b–17 from memory.

   ....
   ....
   ....
   ....
   ....

LESSON 2
Trials and Disappointments

"He got some and I didn't."

"All my friends are doing it."

"That's not fair!"

As children, we were concerned with our rights and with getting our fair share. We were easily bent out of shape if we did not immediately get our way. Do we ever outgrow this mindset? As youth and adults, we can still find ourselves let down, disappointed, and depressed. We are naturally selfish, focusing on ourselves and what we think we deserve. If we are focused on ourselves, we can find many occasions to feel hurt, to become bitter, and to blame God.

Maybe you remember your parents telling you, "Life's not fair." This common saying holds an important truth—we do not all receive the same experiences and treatment. We have different personalities, gifts, and responsibilities.

God's justice means He is perfectly impartial. He does not discriminate between people based on race, gender, or social standing, and He cannot be bribed. However, this does not mean He treats everyone the same. He knows the exact motives and needs of each person, and He gives each of us what is best, even if it is not what we think we deserve. The world does not revolve around us, and not everything that happens will bring us pleasure.

From a human perspective, Joseph had every right to question the goodness of God. Considering the awful things that were done to him, what enabled him to become better instead of bitter?

In this lesson, we will look at how troubles piled up for Joseph. How did he respond? Did he lash out at others or blame God?

Satan will use circumstances to destroy us, but God uses the very same trials to build us and establish us.

EXERCISES

‹ Analyzing God's Word ›

Read Genesis 37, 39, and 40; then complete the following exercise.

1. List the disappointments Joseph faced.

   ....

   ....

   ....

2. Circle the things Joseph could control.

   a. The time and place of his birth
   b. The clothes he was given
   c. What his brothers thought of him
   d. How his brothers treated him
   e. His attitude toward his brothers
   f. Where he was sold
   g. Who his master was
   h. Which gods he worshipped
   i. What jobs he was given
   j. How he did his work
   k. Whether he would give in to sin
   l. Whether he was imprisoned
   m. How he treated the other prisoners
   n. Whether he became bitter

Building Your Word Knowledge

What Rights Do We Deserve?

Write your thoughts.

1. What is a *right*?

2. Make a list of some things that we consider our rights—things we think we deserve.

3. Considering our sins against God and others, what do we really deserve? (Ezra 9:13)

4. Read Romans 6:23. What is the difference between a wage and a gift?

5. Who is the focus of our pleasure seeking? Who are we usually thinking of when we demand fairness?

6. Define *bitterness*:

7. Define *self-pity:*
   ....
   ....

8. Define *contentment:*
   ....
   ....

9. Should we demand only "good" things in our lives?
   ....
   ....

10. What is your real purpose for being here?
    ....
    ....

◀ Comparing Scripture with Scripture ▶

God proves our character by sending us through the heat like gold to be purified. Can God trust us to faithfully handle tough situations? When God tests the eternal value of our character, will it last? (Malachi 3:3; 1 Peter 1:7; 1 Corinthians 3:12–13)

Smelting Gold

Match the beginnings and endings of these verses.

Beginnings

1. .... "Shall we receive good at the hand of God,
2. .... "Blessed are they that mourn:
3. .... "Blessed are they which are persecuted for righteousness' sake:
4. .... "For a just man falleth seven times,
5. .... "The fear of man bringeth a snare:
6. .... "Woe unto him
7. .... "Hath not the potter power
8. .... "Nay but, O man,
9. .... "Shall the thing formed say to him that formed it,

Endings

a. who art thou that repliest against God?" (Romans 9:20a)
b. Why hast thou made me thus?" (Romans 9:20b)
c. but whoso putteth his trust in the LORD shall be safe" (Proverbs 29:25).
d. for they shall be comforted" (Matthew 5:4).
e. that striveth with his Maker!" (Isaiah 45:9)
f. and riseth up again" (Proverbs 24:16).
g. for theirs is the kingdom of heaven" (Matthew 5:10).
h. over the clay . . . ?" (Romans 9:21).
i. and shall we not receive evil?" (Job 2:10)

Write your thoughts.

10. Read Psalm 105:17–19. Who was it that tried Joseph?

....

11. Why does God allow trials to come into our lives?

....

....

12. Does God enjoy hurting us?

....

....

13. The book of 1 Peter discusses suffering and trials. In 1 Peter 2:21–23, we see how Jesus responded under false accusations. 1 Peter 4:12–16 describes how we should respond to suffering. How did Joseph suffer?

....

....

14. Write 1 Peter 2:20 in your own words:

....

....

‹ Strength in Hard Times ›

Fill in the blanks.

15. Nahum 1:7

    "The LORD is good, a .... in the day of ....;
    and he .... them that trust in him."

16. Proverbs 18:10

    "The name of the LORD is a ....: the righteous runneth into it,
    and is ...."

17. Psalm 20:7

    "Some trust in ...., and some in horses: but .... will remember the
    name of the LORD our God."

18. Psalm 46:1

    "God is our refuge and strength, a very .... in trouble."

19. Psalm 27:10

    "When my father and my mother forsake me, then the LORD will ...."

20. Hebrews 13:5

    "I will never .... thee, nor forsake thee."

‹ False Accusations ›

Write your thoughts.

21. Our pride is hurt when we are blamed for something we did not do. We want everyone to know we are innocent. What did Jesus do in such a case? (See Isaiah 53:7)

    ....
    ....
    ....
    ....

22. Did Jesus promise an easy life if we follow Him? (See Matthew 5:11–12; John 15:20)

    ....
    ....
    ....

‹ Discussing and Pondering ›

‹ The Sting of Rejection ›

When we face rejection and injustice, we struggle with many questions. Isn't God paying attention? Is this situation out of His control? Why does He let me suffer like this? Where is He when I'm hurting?

Don't give up. Keep trusting! God made the night so that we can learn to trust Him. God is with us in our pain. Jesus became a man, so He identifies with us. Ultimately, the most important question is, "Do you still trust God?"

Write your thoughts.

1. Have there been times when you were treated extremely unfairly? Did others let you down? How did you react?

   ....
   ....
   ....

2. What do you wish you had done differently?

....

....

....

3. Have you felt betrayed even by God? (See Psalm 22:1, 24; Matthew 27:46)

....

....

....

‹ The Sovereignty of God ›

The Bible teaches that we can give thanks in every situation, knowing that everything God sends is for our good—even the hard times. (Romans 8:28) He does not owe us an apology for allowing hardship in our lives, because it is in hard times that we grow and develop character. Can we see these times as gifts for our good?

"Don't waste good problems." —Otto Koning

Think back to something difficult you experienced. What lessons did you learn? Did you grow through the experience? Do you still wish it had not happened?

Like Joseph, we must learn to see the plan of God in our lives. Joseph had a dream when he was seventeen, revealing that God had a plan for his life. As he clung to that promise for the next twenty years through extreme trials, God was preparing him to save his family. Joseph never could have worked this out on his own.

Circle the correct answer.

4. Who or what orders our life and destiny?

   God   the stars   our wits

5. Is there such a thing as chance or happenstance?

   yes   no   not sure

6. God not only allows things to happen, but He also .... them.

   panics over   orchestrates   ignores

7. He is molding our .... through these very tests.

   character   weight   self-reliance

8. God not only cares when we go through hard times; He also .... to walk with us through them.

   forgets   doesn't want   promises

9. Most of all, He does not give us more than we can .... (1 Corinthians 10:13; Psalm 103: 13–14).

        push   handle   scream

Write your thoughts.

10. God is the Almighty—unlimited in authority, power, and influence. How can trusting in His providence and sovereignty change your life?

....
....
....
....
....

11. What are some ways trials can be valuable?

....
....
....

12. Read Romans 8:28–29. Whose purpose is God working out through the events of our lives?

....

13. Into whose image does God want to mold us?

....

"Every miracle in the Bible is preceded by a problem. If you have no problem, you get no miracle!" —John Maxwell

‹ Engaging Yourself—Memorization and Application ›

Like an insect crawling among the fibers of a tapestry, we cannot see the design God is weaving in our lives. We might even be on the back side of the work. We must remember that the reality is greater than the obstacles surrounding us and that God controls the bigger picture.

‹ Facing Disappointments with Courage ›
- Rejoicing is the greatest weapon against discouragement. Praise in difficulty glorifies God the most (Psalm 107:22; Hebrews 13:15).
- Look for the good.
- Give thanks for what you have.
- Be content to be faithful in the present.

- Serve others. Use your pain to bless others.
- Hold on to the promises and the faithfulness of God.

Write your thoughts.

1. What trial are you facing? Can you be thankful to God and trust Him to work it out for His good?

   ....
   ....
   ....

2. Is there a person in your life who has caused you grief? Consider how Joseph would have responded, and try to come up with a plan to trust God and make a difference for good.

   ....
   ....
   ....
   ....

‹ Bible Memory ›

Follow the directions.

3. On the blanks below, write James 1:2–4.
4. Highlight who this passage is addressed to, and the word *ye*.
5. Underline all the verbs (actions).
6. Circle the remaining nouns.

   ....
   ....
   ....
   ....

7. Now say the verses aloud, emphasizing the words that stand out to you.

‹ Quiz 2 ›

Answer *True* or *False*.

1. *Fairness* means treating everyone exactly the same. ....

2. We deserve God's mercy, since we are basically good. ....

Write the answer in the blank.

3. Where was Joseph sold as a slave by his brothers? ....

4. Why was Joseph thrown into prison? ....

Fill in the blank to complete the sentence or answer the question.

5. God does not merely allow things to happen, He also .... them.

6. God is like a .... with the right to mold and use us as He sees fit.

7. It is our .... that is hurt when we are blamed for something we think we did not do.

8. Where is God when I hurt? ....

9. Hebrews 13:5 says, "I will never leave thee, nor .... thee."

10. Write James 1:2–4 from memory.

....
....
....
....
....
....

LESSON 3
Respect, Honor, and Obedience

Respect for authority is a character quality God honors highly. However, it seems to be diminishing in modern Western society, having given way to a focus on personal pleasure and fulfillment.

When we see people who lack respect toward bosses, police officers, or church leaders, we can assume that they also had a poor relationship with their parents. Respect and honor are developed early in life. Those who are respected by others have first learned to show respect.

Joseph maintained an attitude of respect and obedience throughout his life. His experiences with authority began as a son of his father; then as a slave to Potiphar; then as a prisoner; and finally, as second-in-command to Pharaoh. Both as a son and as a slave, Joseph found freedom by willingly serving those in authority over him—even when their demands did not seem to be in his best interest.[1] There is blessing in obeying even harsh or unfair authorities.

Consider the authorities in your life. Do you long to be free of their control? Do you chafe at what they want you to do? This could be the very thing God turns around for your good and His glory!

Joseph never grew too big to be humble. Genesis 48:12 tells how Joseph, when he brought his two sons to be blessed by his father, bowed with his face to the earth. Even as a great ruler, he humbled himself before his father and his father's God.

EXERCISES

‹ Analyzing God's Word ›

Read Genesis 37 and 39–41; then answer the questions below.

1. Who were the authorities Joseph encountered throughout his life?
   ....
   ....

2. How did Joseph handle his responsibility as a shepherd?
   ....
   ....

3. Could Joseph choose who was in authority over him?

   ....

4. What was Joseph's attitude toward authority? Did he grumble or complain about authority figures?

   ....

   ....

5. How did Joseph talk to and about authority figures?

   ....

   ....

6. Did Joseph obey promptly?

   ....

7. Did he do his work thoroughly?

   ....

8. Were people in authority pleased with Joseph?

   ....

9. Who blessed Joseph's life and work?

   ....

10. Was Joseph primarily concerned with his own welfare and rewards?

    ....

11. Did Joseph demand justice or seek to "even the score" with those who wronged him? Did he "go on strike" to get his message heard?

    ....

    ....

‹ Building Your Word Knowledge ›

Consider the word definitions; then write each word next to the Bible character connected with that behavior.

- Honor—to revere, fix a value upon, make heavy (worth much)
- Respect—to regard with pleasure, have a high opinion of, look intently at, favor
- Obey (be subject to)—to hear intently, heed, submit to authority, listen to a command, carry out a command

- Despise—to show contempt, scorn, reject, esteem little, look down on, consider worthless
- Profane—to defile, desecrate, pollute, wound or stain, disrespect
- Curse—to revile, make light of, despise, speak evil of
- Rebel—to resist, provoke, disobey

1. Balak .... (Numbers 22:10–12)

2. God .... (Genesis 4:4)

3. Children of Israel .... (Deuteronomy 1:23–32)

4. Hagar .... (Genesis 16:5)

5. Jesus .... (Luke 2:51)

6. King Ahasuerus .... (Esther 6:3–6)

7. The nobles of Judah .... (Nehemiah 13:16–18)

‹ What Is Obedience? ›

Honor is more than lip service. It begins in the heart and is displayed in our actions. If a command is not carried out quickly, completely, and cheerfully, it is not true obedience.

Fill in the blanks.

8. "Do all things without murmurings and ...." (Philippians 2:14).

9. "This people draweth nigh unto me with their mouth, and honoureth me with their ....; but their heart is far from me" (Matthew 15:8).

Like two sides of the same coin, honor and obedience are closely linked.

One side is the attitude.   **The other side is the action.**

Obedience without honor or respect is incomplete. Our honor is shown by our actions.

10. "My son, give me thine ...., and let thine eyes observe my ways" (Proverbs 23:26).

Comparing Scripture with Scripture

Complete the crossword puzzle with words from the Scriptures that tell us whom we should honor.

DOWN
1. Fathers of our .... (Hebrews 12:9)
3. Preferring ....
   (Romans 12:10)
4. White with age (Leviticus 19:32)
5. All-knowing one (3 words: 1 Timothy 1:17)
8. Father of .... (Hebrews 12:9)
9. .... powers (Romans 13:1, 7–8)
10. Lord of armies (Malachi 1:6)
12. Those over their servants (1 Timothy 6:1)
16. Guest or foreigner (Zechariah 7:9–10)
18. God's provided sacrifice (Revelation 5:13)
20. Aged person (Leviticus 19:32)

ACROSS
1. Head of the home (Ephesians 6:2)
2. Fellowship of believers (1 Peter 2:17)
6. Container—one's own body (1 Thessalonians 4:4)
7. Everyone (1 Peter 2:17)
9. Bridegroom (Ephesians 5:33)
11. A national ruler (1 Peter 2:17)
12. The one who bore you (Deuteronomy 5:16)
13. God the Father honored this person (John 8:54)
14. A weaker vessel and an heir of grace (1 Peter 3:7)
15. Church leaders (1 Timothy 5:17)
17. To have control (Hebrews 13:17)
19. Preceded in death by their husbands (1 Timothy 5:3–5)

‹ lesson 3 › Respect, Honor, and Obedience   31

The Blessing of the Fifth Commandment

The fifth commandment is noteworthy as the only command with a specific blessing attached to it (Exodus 20:12). The same command also comes with a curse for disobedience (Deuteronomy 27:16; Proverbs 20:20).

When children reach adulthood, they are no longer under the direct authority of their parents. You may not obey every wish of your parents after you are grown, but you are never released from the responsibility to honor your father and mother.

Fill in the blanks to complete the reasons you should honor your parents.

1. Ephesians 6:1–3 – "That it may be ………………………………… with thee, and thou mayest live ………………………………… on the earth." (This is a promise of continuing posterity, not a promise that all children who honor their parents will grow to be old.)

2. Proverbs 3:2 – "………………………………… of days, and long …………………………………, and …………………………………, shall they add to thee." (Honoring your parents prolongs your life by protecting you from destructive foolishness.)

3. Proverbs 3:4 – "So shalt thou find ………………………………… and good ………………………………… in the sight of God and man."

Discussing and Pondering

Showing Respect

We show respect to someone by how we talk *to* them, how we talk *about* them, and the *titles* we use to *refer to* them.

Write your answers in the blanks.

1. When Israel sent Joseph to his brothers in Shechem, Joseph did not say "Why don't you send someone else?" Rather, he said, "…………………………………." (Genesis 37:13)

2. How did Joseph refer to Potiphar in Genesis 39:8? What title did he give him? …………………………………

3. When Joseph was questioning his brothers, he referred to his father as the "old man" they had spoken of (Genesis 43:27). Was he being derogatory or disrespectful? …………………………………

Disrespect Hurts You

When you dishonor and disrespect someone else, such as your parents, you dishonor yourself. When you trash others, you lower your own value, both in your own mind and in the eyes of others. Disrespectful people may think they are being smart and funny, and they may get laughs from others, but they are not respected.

Disrespectful, mocking people are not trusted by their superiors. Potiphar gave Joseph great responsibility because he could trust Joseph to care for his possessions and build a team spirit among the servants he oversaw.

Disrespect toward those you resent is also self-destructive. When you refuse to forgive and honor others, you chain yourself, sometimes for years, to the very person you hate and wish you could forget. Bitterness and anger produce real damage to your health and immunity and shorten your life.[2]

Respect Toward Those Under You

Is it true that it is unnecessary to honor and respect those who are weaker than you or who hold a lower position? *No!* We should honor people, who are made in God's image, no matter who they are (James 2:8–9). Treat each person as a valuable individual! You earn appreciation and influence by treating those who rank below you with love and respect, rather than demeaning and controlling them. Listen to them and value their ideas.

Honor and humility go together. You honor others by laying aside your own desire for honor. Jesus did this when He washed His disciples' feet (John 13:12–15; Matthew 20:25–28).

Read the references given and complete the exercise.
Ephesians 5:25, 28, 33; Colossians 3:21; Ephesians 6:9; Colossians 4:1; Proverbs 14:31

4. List some people who are weaker or of lower status than you, whom you can bless, serve, and honor.

....

....

‹ Tough Questions ›

Write your thoughts.

5. What should you do when someone in authority tells you to do something morally wrong? Does being obedient mean you must do whatever you're told without question?

....

....

....

6. Does submitting to someone make you less important than that person?

....

7. Are you called to respect people who are wrong? What if they have hurt you or failed to protect you? Do you still need to honor them?

....

....

8. Is there anyone you find hard to honor and respect?

....

....

9. Is honor something others must earn before you give it?

....

Engaging Yourself—Memorization and Application

The Power of the Tongue

You can affirm people by telling them what they do well and pointing out God-like qualities they display. "People are influenced by those who praise them."[3] Timing is important; people do not usually hear instruction when we are taking them to task for a fault, and reproving someone who is not listening is a waste of time. However, people *do* listen to those who affirm them.

Most of us are good at spotting faults in others but slow to acknowledge excellence. When was the last time you "caught" someone doing well and commended them? We need to cultivate the habit of building others up instead of tearing them down.

Affirming others is different from flattery. Flattery is speaking well of someone in order to get something in return. Affirmation, on the other hand, is just telling the truth about the good you see in someone, without seeking anything in exchange.

Jon Kropf

How Do We Show Honor?

Too many people spend their lives despising those above them and looking down on those below them. However, we do not live merely for ourselves. We honor others when we reach out to help them and when we humbly accept their help.

Write your thoughts.

1. How can you honor someone in your life today? What does honor look like?

   ....
   ....

2. What are some things you can do to show respect to your parents and make them feel honored?

   ....
   ....
   ....

3. List and discuss some common courtesies and manners we can display in our homes and society.

   ....
   ....
   ....

4. Memorize 1 Peter 2:18. Then write it from memory in the space below.

   ....
   ....
   ....
   ....

‹ Whom Should We Honor? ›

Think about the people God wants us to honor. Jesus said, "If ye love them which love you, what thank have ye?" (Luke 6:32). In the memory verse you wrote on the previous page, underline the words that describe people who are easy to honor. Circle the word describing those who are much more difficult to honor.

‹ Quiz 3 ›

Answer *True* or *False*.

1. Joseph did not need to honor Potiphar since he did not choose to be Potiphar's slave. ....

2. We need to respect only those who are more powerful than we are. ....

3. Flattery is motivated by a selfish desire to get something in return. ....

4. If people laugh when you mock others, it must be okay. ....

Write the answers.

5. Which of the Ten Commandments is the first one with a promise?

6. What did Joseph, the ruler of Egypt, do in the presence of his father when he took his sons to be blessed?

7. What did Jesus do to demonstrate service to others?

Complete the sentences.

8. Obedience is not complete without ....

9. Matthew 15:8 tells us that it is possible to honor someone with our mouth, while our .... is far from him.

10. Write 1 Peter 2:18 from memory.

‹ lesson 3 › Respect, Honor, and Obedience

LESSON 4

Moral Purity

Many people fall when they are alone. If you find yourself in a place where no one you know is present to make sure you are doing right, what will you do? What will keep you faithful to what you know is right if you can gain acceptance by doing wrong? In a new place, no one expects you to abide by the rules where you came from, and your new friends want you to be like them. Your family will not know if you are living right, so the decision is up to you. When in Rome, you can do as the Romans do.

Joseph faced this test. He was taken from his home, his family, his religion, and everything else familiar, and dropped into a whole new life. In Egypt, no one knew him. No one expected him to live as he had been taught.

In Egypt, it may even have been dangerous for Joseph to hang on to his old beliefs. The Egyptians did not fear the true God. Egypt had different gods and different morals. If Joseph sinned against his God, no one around him would know or care.

EXERCISES

‹ Analyzing God's Word ›

Read Genesis 39 and write your thoughts.

1. List some things that could have made it hard for Joseph to do what was right.

   ....

2. How old do you think Joseph was during the time he served Potiphar? ....

3. Do you think life was better for Joseph in Potiphar's house than living at home with his brothers?

   ....

4. Why do you think Potiphar's wife's offer could have been attractive?

   ....

   ....

5. Did Joseph want what Potiphar's wife offered? Why or why not?

6. How did Joseph respond to his master's wife's attempt to seduce him?

7. What did Joseph do when he found himself cornered?

8. How was Joseph's uprightness rewarded by his master?

9. How was Joseph's uprightness rewarded by God?

10. When Joseph was falsely accused, did anyone stand up for him and stop the injustice?

11. Did Joseph give up on serving God and doing right?

‹ Building Your Word Knowledge ›

‹ What Is Integrity? ›

English Definition
The following definitions are compiled from several sources:
- Possession of, and adherence to, high moral principles or professional standards
- Quality or state of being complete, unimpaired, undamaged, or undivided; being pure or genuine

Hebrew and Greek Definitions
Strong's Exhaustive Concordance is a valuable resource for finding all the references for any word in the KJV Bible. Each Scripture reference also includes a number linking that instance of the English word to the Hebrew or Greek word from which it was translated.

Strong's uses the KJV spellings, such as "honour" instead of "honor." The Hebrew and Greek dictionaries appear in the back section of *Strong's*. Be careful to look up a meaning from the correct dictionary (Old Testament

Hebrew or New Testament Greek).

The typeface and the reference number will tell you whether to look up the word in the Hebrew or Greek dictionary. For example, Hebrew reference numbers may be in standard type, preceded by an H or a zero, depending on your edition (8537, H8537, or 08537). Greek reference numbers may appear in *italics*, preceded by a G, or in simple form, depending on your edition (*703*, G703, or 703).

You will need a *Strong's Concordance* to complete the following exercises.

To learn how a concordance works, look up and read 1 Kings 9:4; then find that Scripture reference listed under *integrity* in *Strong's*. Next to the verse listing, you will find the Hebrew reference number 08537. In the Old Testament Hebrew dictionary, you will find a listing that looks something like the following:

08537. תֹּם tôm, tome; from 08552; completeness; figuratively, prosperity; usually (morally) innocence:—full, integrity, perfect(-ion), simplicity, upright(-ly, -ness), at a venture.

The parts of this listing are as follows:
- The reference number
- The Hebrew word in Hebrew lettering
- The English pronunciation
- The etymology, or word roots. (This tells if the listed word is a primary root word, or if it is taken from another word.)
- The concise meaning, or definition, of the word. This ends with a colon (:).
- Following the colon and dash (:—), there is a list of all the ways the word is translated into English throughout the KJV Bible.

Explore the use of a concordance by completing the following exercises.

1. In the Hebrew dictionary listing above, underline the concise definition; then circle the words that are found in the Bible.

Look up the Hebrew word number 08538 and the Greek number 703. For each word, write down the concise definition, followed by the different ways it is translated in the KJV Bible.

2. **08538** .... :— ....

3. **703** .... :— ....

A Practical Definition

Ultimately, it is what we *do* that shows whether we truly understand integrity. Below are several ways integrity works itself out in real life.

Integrity means:
- Doing what is right when others *aren't* watching. (Are you faithful when you are alone? What is your character like in the dark? Do you ever let down your guard against temptation?)
- Doing what is right when others *are* watching. (How do you act when you think others are noticing you? Do you show off? Do you put on a front around your boss, your friends, or the people in your church?)
- Doing what is right even if you must walk alone. (Are you willing to take a stand?)

Synonyms

Synonyms are words that share the same meaning, or are nearly the same. Dictionaries often list some synonyms along with word definitions. A thesaurus specializes in providing lists of words with similar meanings.

Complete the following exercises.

4. Using a thesaurus or dictionary, find several words that are synonyms to each other, and write them on the line.

   ....

   ....

5. The word *integrity* often appears in the Bible as another word of similar meaning. Make a list of some Bible words you think carry the same meaning as *integrity*.

   ....

   ....

An Integrity Checklist

Write your answers in the blanks.

6. Are you ever truly alone? ....

7. Whom should you seek to please most? ....

8. Are you living only for God's approval? ....

9. Are you committed to doing what is right, no matter what? ....

10. Would you be ashamed if your parents, pastor, or boss found out about things you are doing? ....

"We esteem purity too little and desire it too late." —Josh Harris[4]

Bible Truths About Integrity

Choose one of the following verses to go in the following blanks (one of the blanks takes two verses):

Acts 9:15; James 1:17; 2 Chronicles 16:9; 2 Timothy 2:21

11. Too often people see purity as a nuisance that interferes with their desire for pleasure. In reality, purity is a blessing, unlocking full enjoyment of life. Our Father in heaven is a *giver of good gifts.*

    ....

    ....

12. God not only wants to save us *from* sin and destruction, He wants to save us *for* His special purpose—a life of love, joy, peace, patience, goodness, and self-control.

    ....

    ....

13. The world needs men and women of integrity and virtue, but they are few and far between. God is looking for such people.

....

....

> "The world has yet to see what God can do with and for and through and in and by the man who is fully and wholly consecrated to Him. I will try my utmost to be that man." —D.L. Moody

Will you fill this need?

‹ Joseph's Journal ›

Below are imaginary excerpts from Joseph's journal, his love story as told to his children, and his instructions to the people of his day regarding moral purity. Choose words from the list below to fill in the blanks.

build   choose   avoid   abundant   proper   fuzzy   turn away   intentional   valuable

A Journal Prayer

Heavenly Father,

I love you and know you are with me, yet I feel surrounded by wickedness. I feel that sin is trying to drag me down. There are temptations everywhere in this culture. They war against what I know in my heart you want me to do.

Lately, my master's wife has been enticing me. I have tried to (14) .... her, but that is becoming harder to do. How can I stay away from her when my work takes me through the house so much? I have told her no, but she doesn't give up. She is a beautiful woman, and I must confess that she makes my heart race, but I know she is forbidden. I cannot take what belongs to my master.

I must fight temptations outside and feelings within. Oh, God, I do not want to sin against you. My body belongs to you. Even though others do these things, I will not. I (15) .... the virtues of purity, faithfulness, and obedience that you prize. I commit to closing my eyes and ears and protecting my heart and mind. I will (16) .... my feet from evil. No matter what happens to me or what she threatens, I will be true to you and true to myself. I ask you to be my fulfilment, my love, and my delight. I will not disappoint you.

Your slave, Joseph

Joseph's Love Story

Children,

I am thankful that I can tell you my story without shame, for I kept myself pure and my conscience clear before God.

God created sexuality, and it is good. He designed it pure and beautiful within marriage. You win lasting benefits by denying yourself immediate gratification. Your innocence is a (17) .... gift from God, and there is untold joy and anticipation in waiting until the proper time to open this gift.

Even though I was thrown into prison, God guarded my innocence. On our wedding day, I was able to give your mother my love as an unopened gift. I have never regretted that! As a young man, I longed for love. My heart would pound and my mind would race, but I came to see that these (18) ....

feelings are only emotions and not true love. I found that love is a decision.

There were times when I had to choose to love even when I did not feel it. Don't worry; emotions and feelings follow the choice of committed love.

I chose to love God and trust His timing. I chose to keep myself for the one He would lead me to. In turn, He rewarded me with full emotions and (19)... love.

Joseph's Wisdom on Passion

Your passions and sexuality are like a garden of plenty. A healthy garden requires (20)... planting of the crops you desire. You must cultivate, fertilize, and water a garden if you want it to flourish. Your goal is not merely to keep the garden free of weeds but to enjoy its fruit. You must (21)... up the good, not just root out the bad.

Fire is very useful in an oven or pit, giving warmth and cooking your food. Outside these limits, however, it can become a raging inferno and destroy your home. Our passions are like fire; God has given them for our benefit, and physical intimacy is good in its (22)... place. Yet out-of-control passions bring death. God has placed boundaries for our protection. He limits physical union to the confines of marriage because He loves us.

Cameron Strandberg

‹ Comparing Scripture with Scripture ›

‹ Is It Weak to Flee? ›

Write your thoughts.

You have heard the phrase *fight or flight*.

1. If a prey animal stands and fights a predator, would you consider that animal *strong* or *weak*?

   ....

2. Do you consider an animal that *flees* strong or weak?

   ....

Shutterstock

Here is another way to look at it: for an animal designed with strength and speed to flee, staying to face the predator is not strong, but merely stupid!

Too often we see fleeing as an expression of fear or weakness, and we think it is wimpy to flee. However, 1 Corinthians 10:14–15 says, "Wherefore, my dearly beloved, flee from idolatry. I speak as to wise men; judge ye what I say." Here Paul is speaking to strong men, not weak men, and he tells them to flee from sin. You may think you are strong enough to handle sin, but staying and flirting with sin is foolishness, not strength. To flee is not weak; it is wise!

Consider Eve; rather than flee temptation, she stayed to reason with it. It sounded exciting. She fell because she thought she was strong enough to resist and wise enough to decide right and wrong for herself (Genesis 3).

Remember Joseph; he conquered the temptation to commit immorality because he said no. He considered it great wickedness to sin against God (Genesis 39:9). He would not listen to or even be with Potiphar's wife. He fled at all costs.

"Flee also youthful lusts: but follow righteousness, faith, charity, peace, with them that call on the Lord out of a pure heart" (1 Timothy 2:22).

The source of our power to flee is revealed in James 4:7: "Submit yourselves therefore to God. Resist the devil, and he will flee from you." You cannot resist sin and Satan on your own. To resist temptation, you must first submit yourself to God. He is the one who gives you power to flee, and without His power, you can do nothing.

In 1 Corinthians 10:13, God promises to provide a way of escape from temptation. This way of escape is usually given *early* in the temptation. We have to take God's escape right away. Temptation is a little like traveling on a superhighway—if you miss your exit, you may have to travel a long way before the next opportunity to get off.

Often people say something like, "But I couldn't help myself. The temptation was too strong!" We cannot blame God if we have ignored His warnings and passed the exits He has provided.

Nature teaches us that fleeing is sometimes expedient. Some lizards, when caught by their tails, will shed their tails in order to escape.

Jon Kropf

"Deliver thyself as a roe from the hand of the hunter, and as a bird from the hand of the fowler" (Proverbs 6:5).

Fill in the blanks.

3. "Keep thy heart with all .... ; for out of it are the issues of life" (Proverbs 4:23).

4. Read 1 Peter 5:8. Your very life is at stake! Who is your adversary? ....

In "Building Your Word Knowledge," you listed some Bible words with similar meanings to *integrity*. Now look up each of those words in your concordance and find several verses using that word that could help you withstand temptation. Using the lines below, write the word on the left and Scripture references on the right.

5. ....

‹ Discussing and Pondering ›

‹ Setting Up Protections ›

Circle the correct word to complete each sentence.

1. "Let him that thinketh he standeth take heed lest he ...." (1 Corinthians 10:12).
       run   stand   fall

2. Even if you find the experience exhilarating, you cannot handle .... yourself.
       temptation   food   watching

3. Do not consider the .... of sin by listing its pros and cons. Little steps can gradually lead you away from God.
       idleness   possibility   fear

4. Do not .... your guard. King David fell into sin when he was just "hanging around" (2 Samuel 11).
       cushion   relax   intimidate

5. Beware of the .... glance and the longing look. Adultery begins in the heart (Matthew 5:27–28).
       evil   kind   second

6. Beware of placing yourself in .... situations. Do not allow yourself to be alone with temptation.
       enjoyable   compromising   colorful

7. .... the presence of God with you at all times.
       Welcome   Resent   Fear

8. Realize that the battle for integrity begins in the ....
   deed   mind   magazine

9. Lust thrives on secrecy. Nothing diffuses it like .... your struggle to another person.
   bragging about   confessing   hiding

10. The temptation to lust is always .... There is never a need to gratify or indulge yourself through sin.
    selfish   gentle   giving

Using Caution Online

The use of the Internet, including communication technologies like email, instant messaging, texting, and phone calls can greatly increase your temptation to sin. It is easier than ever to invite someone you know little about into the privacy of your own home or room. Because of the buffer the Internet provides between people, it is easy to say or do things online that you would not say or do in person or in public.

Remember that anything you post online remains on record somewhere even if you erase it. Illicit relationships are damaging anywhere, but they are especially risky online, where a stranger posing as a friend can easily be a sexual predator or someone seeking information to blackmail you later.

If people you don't know well ask you to call or write them, or give you their number, beware. It is not noble or necessary to return a message. If a temptation is "stood up," so what? You do not owe temptation an answer or explanation.

A Foundation of Wisdom

In our world we are bombarded by strong temptations, but it is still possible to stand. If we have our feet firmly planted on the Word of God, we will stand firm. This means not just hearing and knowing what is right, but doing it. Jesus said those who hear and do His words are like a wise man who built his house on a firm foundation that the storms and floods could not erode. Psalm 1 describes the godly person as an established and well-nourished tree.

A Stairway Downward

Immorality is a degrading staircase. If the very bottom step were labeled *sexual perversion,* how would you label the other steps that lead you down? You do not just wake up in sin one day; small choices are the steps that take you down.

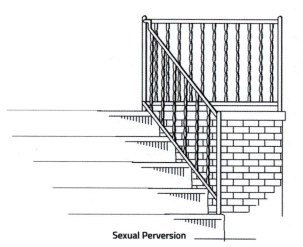

Sexual Perversion

Write your thoughts.

11. What are some ways you have gained victory over temptation?

....

....

Is This Okay?

If you really wonder whether your reading material, the photos and videos you are looking at, or your activities are okay, try checking your heart rate. Does it hammer when you hear someone else coming? Do you find yourself looking over your shoulder to make sure no one is watching you?

‹ Protecting Others ›

Questions to Think About

Can you be trusted with the hearts of others? Do you do all you can to guard their purity, innocence, and morality? Do you help them maintain pure thoughts? We need to have a loving concern for our brothers and sisters. Is there ever a need to experiment before marriage to see if you are compatible? No! Playing with intimacy never brings honor. It only brings guilt and shame.

Do you tempt your friends or wear down their convictions? Never pressure others to give in to temptation. This is unkind and dishonorable behavior, even if you think they are strong enough to resist. True love honors and protects others.[5] People face enough temptations without you adding to the onslaught.

Are you treating this person the way you would want someone to treat your future spouse? Self-control before marriage establishes a basis for a better experience within marriage.

How to Protect

As a young man, you should keep the following points in mind as you associate with women and girls:
- View yourself as the protector, not the hunter.
- Treat your girlfriend or wife as your sister. You are joint-heirs of salvation. You must answer to God for how well you cherish a daughter of the King.
- Do not play with girls' emotions or lead them on. Do what you can to help them guard their hearts and minds. Beautiful flowers are easily crushed.
- Lead by example—love God with all your heart.
- Do not steal their focus from God (Hebrews 10:24).

As a young woman, you have a part in protecting the purity of boys and men.
- Do not try to use your charms to control others. Don't be a flirt.
- Avoid dressing or acting in ways that tempt others to lust. When you buy or make clothes, consider what will glorify God, rather than just what is cute and fashionable.
- You don't have to show off what you have. Keep yourself special.
- Make God the love of your heart.

Write your thoughts.

12. What worth or value would you place on a pure, godly woman? (Proverbs 31:10)

....
....

13. What can you do to value purity more?

....
....
....

14. The seriousness of dealing with sin is expressed by Jesus in Matthew 5:29–30. "If thy right eye offend thee, ... If your hand offends you, ..." Why would these severe actions be better than continuing in sin? ....

‹ Drawing Boundaries ›

Set boundaries for yourself when you are strong, *before* you face temptation. Consider the places and times where you are weakest. Safeguards may be inconvenient, but they are critical in protecting your heart commitment.

Be accountable by letting others know of your commitments. Some people may think you are strange and old-fashioned, but in the end you must give account to God for yourself and your conduct.

Drawing boundaries should not be an end in itself, or even the starting point. To be successful in a life of purity, you must start with a heart desire to please God.[6] A relationship with God is the most important part of a righteous life. Spend time with God daily. Do not rely on your own strength—you will need the power of God to stand.

‹ Engaging Yourself—Memorization and Application ›

1. **Memorize Matthew 5:8; then write it from memory in the blanks below.**

   ....

   ....

   ....

‹ Guarding with Diligence ›

Proverbs 31:11 says of the virtuous woman, "The heart of her husband doth safely trust in her." Single people can honor their marriage partner even before they are married. Trust is built long before you say, "I do," and trust is a gift that must be guarded. Live your life in such a way that your spouse will never have reason to doubt your integrity.

Write your thoughts.

2. List some ways men can guard their hearts.

   ....

   ....

   ....

3. List some ways women can guard their hearts.

   ....

   ....

   ....

4. List some ways couples can protect their relationships.

   ....
   ....
   ....

‹ Quiz 4 ›

Answer *True* or *False*.

1. Lust thrives on secrecy. ....

2. It is fine to reason with temptation, as long as you know what you believe. ....

Fill in the blanks to complete the sentences.

3. To flee is not weak; it is ....!

4. "We esteem .... too little and desire it too late."

5. "The world has yet to see what God can do with and for and through and in and by the man who is fully .... to Him."

6. God not only wants to save us *from* sin and its heartaches, but He wants to save us *for* ....

Answer each question.

7. How was Joseph rewarded for fleeing the advances of Potiphar's wife?

   ....
   ....

8. When is the best time to set your boundaries?

   ....

9. Are we responsible to help protect the hearts of others?

   ....

10. Write Matthew 5:8 from memory.

   ....
   ....
   ....
   ....

LESSON 5
Samson: A Life of Dishonor

As we seek direction for our lives, a key question we should ask is, "What does God want me to do?" Another question we might ask is, "What does Satan want me to do?" Sometimes looking at a negative quality helps us avoid going where we do not want to go. It is wise to learn by watching how others handle the tests of life, instead of learning everything by firsthand experience. Both the triumphs and failures of others have much to teach us.

Samson, like Joseph, was called out for a special purpose—to deliver Israel from its oppressors. He served as a judge in Israel. While we may be impressed by his feats of strength, we cringe when we read of his moral failures. Samson's indulgence in sin limited the effects of God's power in his life. Although forgiveness was available to Samson, we can only wonder what God could have done through him had he followed God with his whole heart.

EXERCISES

Analyzing God's Word

Read Judges 13–16 and answer the following questions.

1. What calling was placed on Samson's life?

   ....

2. What were the signs of his vow?

   ....

   ....

3. Where did Samson's strength come from? (Judges 13:25; 14:6)

   ....

4. What demand of Samson's brought heartache to his parents?

   ....

   ....

5. What emotion controlled Samson when he found out his wife had told his enemies the answer to his riddle?

   ....

6. Samson was intrigued by treading on forbidden ground. He was enamored with immoral women. In which enemy city did he spend the night with a harlot?

   ....

7. Do you think Samson's character qualified him to judge Israel for twenty years?

   ....

8. Did Samson's actions show that he valued his vow of separation?

   ....

9. Whose strength did Samson come to rely on? (Judges 16:20)

   ....

10. When did Samson flee temptation?

    ....

11. What would you say was Samson's greatest bondage?

    ....

    ....

‹ Building Your Word Knowledge ›

‹ What Is Purity? ›

Purity means to be free of pollutants or contamination. To be pure is to be clean and without mixture. Purity also means to be free of moral fault or guilt.

> **"And every man that hath this hope in him purifieth himself, even as he is pure"**
> **(1 John 3:3).**

Write your thoughts.

1. Read the definition of purity again. Imagine you are drawing a picture of something pure. Describe your picture of purity in the space below.

   ....

   ....

   ....

   ....

‹ lesson 5 › Samson: A Life of Dishonor

2. Describe something that has become impure.

....
....
....

‹ God-Given Desires ›

Have you ever wondered why God gives us such strong desires and then forbids indulging them? Does it feel cruel that God gives you longings for intimacy, only to say, "Not yet"?

God has given us the responsibility to protect the gift of physical intimacy. If such a relationship were not desirable, it would not be much of a gift. If there were no anticipation and no pleasure in attainment, we would probably not pursue such a relationship. Sexual union was God's idea; He commanded man and woman to marry and be fruitful. Within God's boundaries of marriage to one partner for life, this relationship is a delightful gift.

When burglars break into a home, what items do they target—the worthless or the valuable? It makes sense, doesn't it, that God's most precious gifts are the things the devil tries hardest to steal, pollute, and destroy?

Write your thoughts.

3. What are some things in our society that have become twisted from what God intended?

....
....
....

‹ A Moral Compass ›

For each sentence below, choose the correct ending. For each choice you make, follow the directions to trace the route on the compass after the questions.

4. Lust is a form of
    a. selfishness. (Begin at A and go south to P)
    b. love. (Begin at A and go east to T)

5. Yearning for what is forbidden is
    a. covetousness. (Travel straight to M)
    b. patience. (Travel straight to F)

6. A fruit of the Spirit listed in Galatians 5:22–23 is
    a. greed. (Go to I)
    b. temperance, or self-control. (Go to B)

7. "Possessing your vessel" in 1 Thessalonians 4:4 refers to
    a. indulging your flesh. (Go to N)
    b. denying your flesh. (Go to Q)

8. Self-gratification is (for a clue, read Ephesians 4:18–19)
    a. selfish, addictive, and often intertwined with fantasy or pornography. (Travel to R)

50 Integrity: A study on the life of Joseph

b. harmless, okay, and something everybody does. (Travel to U)

9. Giving in to temptation will
   a. satisfy you and make the temptation fade away. (Continue to F)
   b. make the temptation stronger. (Continue to Z)

10. Read Ephesians 5:3. Concerning impurity, we should
    a. not allow a hint or suggestion of it in our lives. (Travel to O)
    b. flirt with it. (Travel to X)

11. In my own strength,
    a. I can keep the devil from getting his foot in the door. (Go to S)
    b. I am not strong enough to resist sin. (Go to A)

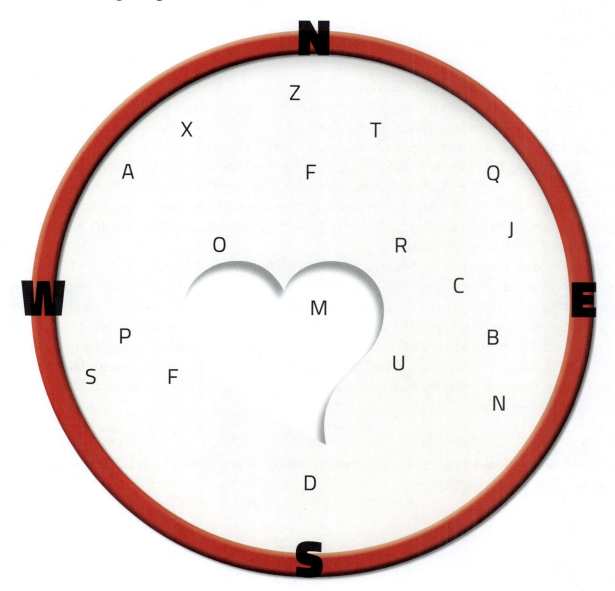

Did you wander aimlessly or was there a purpose? What shape did you draw? ....

James 1:12 says, "Blessed is the man that endureth temptation: for when he is tried, he shall receive the crown of life, which the Lord hath promised to them that love him."

‹ Comparing Scripture with Scripture ›

The battle for your soul and body begins in your mind. One little wrong thought, if you entertain it, becomes two, and soon they attract more, filling your mind and twisting your reality. Before long, you no longer know the difference between right and wrong, and you begin pursuing evil and avoiding good. Samson learned that sin takes you further than you want to go, keeps you longer than you want to stay, and costs you more than you want to pay.

Sow a thought; reap a deed.
Sow a deed; reap a habit.
Sow a habit; reap a character.
Sow a character; reap a destiny.

‹ Beware the Strange Woman! ›

It is important to listen to the wisdom of those who love us and have experienced some of the same temptations we do. King Solomon, who wrote much of the book of Proverbs, often offered practical advice from a parent's perspective. Listen to his voice of wisdom: "My son, if sinners entice thee, consent thou not" (Proverbs 1:10). "Keep thy heart with all diligence; for out of it are the issues of life" (Proverbs 4:23).

A frequent warning in Proverbs is to keep yourself from the "strange woman," who offers fleeting pleasures while dragging your soul to hell. The strange woman is used in Proverbs as a symbol of lust, a warning to avoid anyone, man or woman, who entices us to sin by gratifying our selfish desires. Such people sometimes seem to lurk at every corner.

Strange in the sense in which Proverbs uses it does not necessarily refer to someone who seems abnormal, creepy, or evil. More likely, the strange man or woman will be someone who attracts you. The key characteristic of such a person is that you do not know them well—you are unfamiliar with their habits and intentions.

Many people have been trapped by the idea that they can get away with immorality with a stranger. A "fling" or a relationship with a prostitute is enticing because it offers new and exciting forms of pleasure without accountability. You feel as though you can enjoy yourself with no strings attached. It's easy to imagine that if no one you know finds out what you did, there will be no harmful consequences. But this is a lie, as many people learn too late.

Temptations and Consequences

In the blanks below, write a T next to the temptations and lies of a "stranger," and a C next to the consequences of yielding to temptation.

1. .... Brokenness
2. .... Flattery, enticing looks, flirtations
3. .... Smooth talk
4. .... Shame, or reproach
5. .... Your feet trapped in a net
6. .... Losing your relationship with God

7. .... Affection given freely
8. .... Promises of pleasure
9. .... The chambers of death and hell
10. .... "We won't get caught."
11. .... "I'm available."
12. .... Forbidden things—"Stolen waters are sweet."
13. .... Bitterness
14. .... Rebellious or suggestive language
15. .... Death—a dart through the liver

(Background verses: Deuteronomy 7:3–4; Proverbs 5:3–6; 6:12–15, 23–33; 7:10–23; 9:16–18; 29:5)

When You Sin, You Lose

Proverbs 5:3–13; 6:27–35; 13:15; Romans 6:21–22; Revelation 21:7–8, 23, 27

Consider these consequences of sin and how they could apply to the scenarios below.

feeling unforgiven
painful memories
job loss
destroyed trust
separation from God
addictions

court battles
deadened conscience
unplanned pregnancy
ruined marriages
feeling disqualified
diseases

childlessness
hate and suspicion
child support
single parenting
ruined reputation

Lillian was not pure in college. Now she cannot give herself to her husband or allow him to love her. Regret and shame from the past steal the security, joy, and excitement of marriage from her.

....

It started when one of the girls at work started being suggestive to Philip. At the time, it made him feel like "the man," but now he realizes that he was the fool to play with fire.

....

Karla is struggling to raise a three-year-old daughter by herself after the man who said he loved her dropped out of her life.

....

Todd wishes he had never yielded to immorality. He hasn't been feeling well and has missed over a month of school. The doctor thinks he might have HIV. His friends are embarrassed to talk to him. Some people are afraid to be with him lest they catch something. He feels like an outcast.

....

Travis knows that he shouldn't fill his mind with filth. He knows God is not pleased with his thoughts. He feels dirty, yet he finds himself trapped in a web of immorality, falling for the same sin again and again. When he tries to pray to God, his prayers seem to fall to the floor.

....

Kathy has filled her mind with romance novels. She has a hard time appreciating her boring, unromantic husband. Why doesn't he care more? Recently she found an immoral magazine he had hidden under the mattress. She feels dirty and violated to think he has been gaining satisfaction from other women. But is Kathy really any different?

....

Kim is afraid to tell her fiancé, Carl, that she has a venereal disease from a previous one-time relationship. She now fears she will never be able to have children. Maybe Carl will refuse to marry her when he knows the truth.

....

Levi lives alone in a camp trailer behind his parents' home. Court fees destroyed his once-thriving excavating business. His wife took the house and sold half of his equipment during the divorce. He has no real home in which to keep his children when they stay with him one weekend a month. He can hardly afford to spend time with them, since he is working two jobs to pay for alimony and child support.

....

Stacy and Mark were so "in love" when they were dating that they decided not to wait. But when they finally married, the excitement they had hoped for was missing. Now Stacy has trouble trusting Mark. If he didn't honor her before marriage, what would keep him from being unfaithful now? She is suspicious whenever he comes home late.

....

‹ The Deceitful Heart ›

> **"The heart is deceitful above all things, and desperately wicked: who can know it?" (Jeremiah 17:9)**

Use the word list below to fill in the blanks.

> slave   stop   teasing   small   undermine   better   myself
> mock   nullify   real   consequences   compatible   forfeited

People often play with others' emotions, thinking it is harmless (16) .... When we entice or toy with someone, we are trying to fulfill our desire to feel wanted and loved. Enticing others can give us a sense of control, but it violates the other person.

We tend to think we can (17) .... any time. "I can always turn the temptation off. I'm strong enough to resist."

We easily believe the lie that "sin won't get me; I can escape the (18) ...."

We are deceived if we excuse ourselves by thinking the sin we are involved in is not that serious. Big outbreaks of sin are triggered by unguarded (19) .... sins." We may tell ourselves that pictures or novels are not (20) .... , so they don't qualify as lust or adultery. But it is important to remember that all sin begins in the heart.

One does not need to watch graphic movies to be affected by sin. Even materials that seem only slightly tainted can slowly and subtly (21) .... Biblical truth and conviction in our hearts.[7] Our media and culture mixes good and bad to the point that we can become desensitized without knowing it. An interesting story plot does not (22) .... the poison it carries with it. Ask yourself, "Does this trivialize or glorify sin? Does it (23) .... the things of God?" (See Romans 1:32.)

"My heart lies to me that it is okay to fantasize about things I would never actually do. I keep these thoughts to (24) .... and they hurt no one" (see Proverbs 6:18). It is a mistake to believe our thoughts will not affect others.

Some people think marriage is an open-ended relationship—just an experiment. They want to keep their options open, in case someone (25) .... comes along.[8] End this deception by realizing that saying "I do" to marriage also involves saying no to all other people and options.

Some people insist that you need to experiment before marriage to see if you are (26) ...., but this is not true.[9] You will have a lifetime to learn together.

Our hearts will beg to indulge in sin just once. Indulging is not expressing freedom—it is making ourselves a (27) .... to sin (Romans 6:16).

If we have given in just a little, the next lie says we have gone too far already, so we may as well go all the way. Those who have compromised often feel they have lost the right to say no. They may feel that by being "bad" they have (28) .... their rights to purity, dignity, and honor, and that they now deserve shame.[10] It is wrong to think you cannot say no because you have failed in the past. It is never too late to start walking in righteousness.

‹ Discussing and Pondering ›

‹ How Far Can I Go? ›

If you find yourself asking this question, stop and rethink your focus and priorities. If you are focused on finding out how much you can get by with, you are likely to miss the fulfilling things God is calling you to do. Is your chief desire to do God's will, or is it to find out how much you are allowed to indulge yourself?

Rather than asking, "How far is too far?" we should ask, "How close can I get to God?"

For each question below, circle the answer you think is correct.

1. When does immorality become sin? (Matthew 5:28)
    a. In the heart
    b. In touching
    c. In committing fornication

2. Which is considered sin in the sight of God? (James 1:14–15; Matthew 15:11; 18–20)
    a. Entertaining wrong thoughts or attitudes
    b. Wrong actions
    c. Both

To hit a target, an archer has to aim above it. Likewise, to live a pure life, you must set your standards higher than you may feel is absolutely necessary.[11]

Write your thoughts.

3. Proverbs 6:32 says, "But whoso committeth adultery with a woman lacketh understanding: he that doeth it destroyeth his own soul." How do fornication and adultery destroy a person's soul?

....
....
....

‹ Three Laws of Sowing and Reaping ›

- You reap *what* you sow (Proverbs 28:13; Galatians 6:7–8).
- You reap *more than* you sow (Hosea 8:7).
- You reap *later than* you sow.

‹ Too Late for Purity? ›

Lori has confessed her sin to God, and she knows she is forgiven, but she has a hard time feeling cleansed. Resisting temptation seems much harder since she lost her purity. Becoming purified through God's grace is wonderful, but it is hard to really feel as though she has something to keep as a treasure now. The devil whispers, "It's too late to make a stand. You can never recover."

Can innocence ever be regained? Can you be a virgin again? Yes, although you may still face consequences for wrongs done in the past, you can start over, and you can be pure.

It is never too late to stop taking poison. Start by asking God to cleanse your subconscious thoughts; then stop feeding your mind with garbage.

Philippians 4:8 describes the kinds of things we should fill our minds with. If your mind is full of these, will there be room for anything else?

4. Write Philippians 4:8 below.

....
....
....
....

Is there some sin you cannot forgive yourself for? Whatever that sin is, it is not the worst thing you have done. No, the worst thing you have done is to be responsible for the death of God's Son. Your sin nailed Jesus to the cross. Yet God forgives that great sin. What amazing grace!

You deserved death for your sin, but Jesus took your place, and now God offers you forgiveness. God's mercy and forgiveness is based on His faithfulness and goodness, not yours.[3] (Romans 8:1; Isaiah 1:18; Psalms 103:10–12; Isaiah 43:25)

2 Corinthians 5:17 says we can become a new creation in Christ. That is why salvation is called a *new birth*. No matter what we have done in the past, Christ gives us freedom to walk in victory! Hallelujah!

‹ Engaging Yourself—Memorization and Application ›

‹ Galatians 6:7–8 ›

There is a useful Bible memorization tool called "illustrated writing." It consists of drawing simple pictures or arranging letters to illustrate a thought. This focuses your mind on the meaning and helps the words stick in your mind. While it takes some creativity, you do not need to be an artist to do it. Not every verse will lend itself to this memory tool, but some are fun. Below is an example of 2 Corinthians 10:5 drawn in illustrated writing.

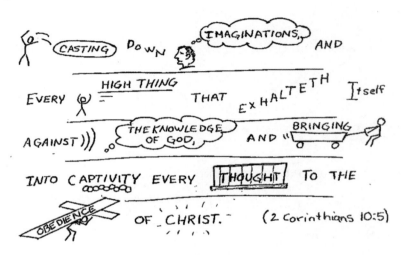

1. In the space below, write out Galatians 6:7–8 in illustrated writing while memorizing it.

‹ A Fresh Start ›

2. **Write out a personal prayer of purity to God. Ask Him for cleansing and a fresh start. Ask Him for daily strength to be pure. Believe that with His help, you can be a man of honor or a woman of virtue!**

....
....
....
....
....

Quiz 5

Answer *True* or *False*.

1. If I confess my sin, all the consequences of my sin will be taken away. ....

2. If you have lost your virginity, it is too late for you to be pure. ....

Write the answer in the blanks.

3. Did Samson value his vow of separation? ....

4. Samson was intrigued with treading on .... ground. Did he *embrace* or *flee* temptation? ....

Complete the quotes.

5. "My son, if sinners entice thee, ..."

6. "Sow a thought; reap a deed. Sow a deed; reap a .... Sow a ....; reap a character. Sow a character; reap a destiny."

Fill in the blanks to complete the statements.

7. .... means "without pollutant or contamination; clean and without mixture."

8. People who commit adultery lack .... and destroy their own ....

9. Instead of asking, "How far can I go and still be pure?" we should ask, ... ?

10. Write Galatians 6:7–8 from memory.

....
....
....
....
....
....

LESSON 7
Preparing for Famine

Have you ever had to save money for a need you saw coming? Saving is wise and responsible, and waiting to purchase something until you can pay for it is a good exercise in patience.

Modern American society has made us so used to getting what we want immediately that it's hard for us to wait. We are prone to selfishness, and it is easy to forget that the Lord's Prayer teaches us to pray for our basic needs—not just our wants.

In today's lesson, God revealed in a dream that He was sending seven years of abundance followed by seven years of extreme famine. How would you prepare if you knew you would soon face seven years of drought and food shortages? Would you begin planning right away, or would you wait a few years? Would you begin by stockpiling provisions for yourself? Would you think of others also?

In the year 1999, many people feared that a computer glitch known as the Y2K bug would cause widespread failure of computer systems as the year rolled over to 2000. Some people predicted massive power failures and food shortages as computer-controlled power plants and distribution centers shut down. Many people stockpiled food, guns, and ammunition to protect themselves against a collapse, and most had no intention of sharing their stores with anyone else.

Experts worked hard to try to patch vulnerable systems, but the work was far from finished when 2000 finally arrived—and little happened. Most of the predictions had been merely hype.

In contrast, Joseph's warning of a coming famine was not based on suppositions or educated guesswork. It was a reality, a warning given by God; and he, Joseph, was commissioned to save the nations.

EXERCISES

‹ Analyzing God's Word ›

Read Genesis 40:20–41:57 and answer the following questions.

1. How long was Joseph forgotten by Pharaoh's butler? ....

2. How does it feel when someone forgets to keep a promise he or she made to you?

....

3. What three sets of dreams have we discussed during the study of Joseph's life?

....

....

....

4. Who did Joseph say would give Pharaoh an "answer of peace"? ....

5. Who would be affected if Joseph's interpretation came true? ....

6. Why did Pharaoh believe Joseph? ....

7. When did Joseph begin to save for the famine? ....

8. When did the famine arrive? ....

9. Who were the stored provisions for? ....

10. Who unexpectedly came to buy grain from Joseph? ....

‹ Building Your Word Knowledge ›

Match the related words.

1. .... prosperity   a. covetousness
2. .... greed   b. starvation and debt
3. .... famine   c. duty
4. .... store   d. save
5. .... slothful   e. industrious
6. .... stewardship   f. lazy
7. .... diligent   g. earthly treasures

8. **Look up the references that contain the words *slothful* and *sluggard* in Proverbs. You can use a topical Bible or concordance. Pick two or three verses that speak to you, and write them on the lines below.**

....

....

....

....

....

....

‹ lesson 7 › Preparing for Famine

‹ Industry versus Laziness ›

Match the word pictures to the references.

9. .... Proverbs 6:6–11 illustrates industriousness using
10. .... Proverbs 18:9 compares the slothful person to
11. .... Proverbs 24:30–34 compares the life of a lazy person to

a. an overgrown garden
b. someone who "wastes," or destroys
c. an ant

There is a saying, "If you want something done, look for a busy person." People who are making the most of what they have are entrusted with greater responsibility (Luke 16:10–11).

"His lord said unto him, Well done, thou good and faithful servant: thou hast been faithful over a *few* things, I will make thee ruler over *many* things: enter thou into the joy of thy lord" (Matthew 25:21).

‹ Comparing Scripture with Scripture ›

‹ Is Wealth Wrong? ›

Jesus did not teach against storing up for the future; He taught against storing wealth here on earth, where it will pass away. Investing in perishable goods is foolish. On the contrary, Jesus commands us to invest in heavenly treasures that last forever.[16]

Earthly Riches versus True Riches

Read the passages to find the answers to the questions.

1. Proverbs 23:5 – What do riches make for themselves? ....

2. 1 Peter 1:4 – The believer's inheritance is reserved in heaven. What three things cannot happen to it?
   ....

3. 1 Peter 5:4 – When will believers receive their unfading crown of glory?
   ....
   ....

4. Luke 16:10–14 – Can we focus on collecting the treasures of the kingdom of God and the kingdom of this world at the same time?
   ....

5. 2 Corinthians 9:6–11 – What kind of giver is God pleased with? Does God bless someone living at half–throttle?
   ....

62 Integrity: A study on the life of Joseph

6. Matthew 6:19–20 – Which of these is an unstable investment—*treasures on earth* or *treasures in heaven*?
   ....

7. Matthew 6:21 – Did Jesus say "your treasure is where your heart is" or "your heart is where your treasure is"? What is the difference?
   ....
   ....

8. How do we get our hearts in the right place?
   ....
   ....

9. Mark 10:23–27 – Although all things are possible with God, how likely is the person who is captured by riches to enter the kingdom of God?
   ....
   ....

10. Mark 10:24 and 1 Timothy 6:17 – Is there a difference between having riches and trusting in them?
    ....

11. Luke 12:16–21 – For whom did the rich fool think he was laying up treasure? ....

12. Who do you think might have ended up enjoying the rich fool's wealth?
    ....

Read 1 Corinthians 6:18, 1 Corinthians 10:14, 2 Timothy 2:22, and 1 Timothy 6:11; then write your answers to the questions below.

13. What action verb do the above four verses have in common? ....

14. Does the action verb mean something different in 1 Timothy 6:11 than in the other passages? ....

15. What things are warned against in 1 Timothy 6:6–11, 17–19?
    ....

‹ The Snare of Covetousness ›

Whom are we usually worried about when we invest or save for a rainy day? As you plan for your financial future, are you thinking selfishly, focused only on yourself and your family, or are you thinking of how you can help others too?

Underline the correct word or phrase in parentheses to complete these statements.

16. Luke 12:15 – We need to beware of covetousness, because life is not made up of (friendships; the abundance of things; going to church).

17. 1 Timothy 6:6–11 – Godliness with contentment is (great gain; much pain; worldly fame).

18. Hebrews 13:5 – Be content (once you get a little more; with what you have; with a million dollars).

19. Ephesians 5:3 – Covetousness (is a natural response; is not as bad as immorality; should not be named once among Christians).

20. Colossians 3:5 – Covetousness should be seen as (idolatry; theft; hate).

‹ Preparing for the Future ›

God gave Pharaoh the same dream twice to emphasize the importance of the message. This principle suggests that we should take special note of repeated warnings in the Scriptures. The following proverb is found twice in the book of Proverbs:

> "A prudent man foreseeth the evil, and hideth himself; but the simple pass on, and are punished" (Proverbs 22:3 and Proverbs 27:12).

Preparing for eternity is critical! To spend a lifetime storing up for retirement, only to die without having prepared for life after death, is lunacy. "For what is a man profited, if he shall gain the whole world, and lose his own soul? or what shall a man give in exchange for his soul?" (Matthew 16: 26).

‹ Being Financially Responsible ›

In some ways, financial stability is like a narrow road with a ditch on either side. We should neither sit around waiting for a handout (laziness) nor accumulate things for our own enjoyment or protection (selfishness). Jesus Christ cares how we use our talents and possessions, and He does not endorse either hoarding or laziness (Matthew 25:14–30). We must be wise and frugal with the possessions entrusted to us. Wealth is not a mark of godliness, but neither is poverty.

Holiness is more than voluntary poverty. Giving away your possessions can help you cut loose from worldly concerns, but it will not automatically make you holy (1 Corinthians 13:3). There is wisdom in the prayer of Proverbs 30:8: "Give me neither poverty nor riches."

We need a joy that is independent of how much we own, and a true heart to serve others. When we have this mindset, we will not be satisfied to live *within* our means; we will intentionally live *below* our means in order to share with others (Ephesians 4:28).

Write some practical steps you can take now to become financially responsible.

21. ....
....
....
....
....
....

‹ Lean Times ›

You will not always be the one giving to others; sometimes you will be obligated to others. 1 Corinthians 7:21–22 tells us it is not wrong to be a servant, but it may be an advantage to be free. In the same way, there is nothing wrong with accepting help from others as long as we keep certain truths in mind.

Read the verses below about dealing with obligations; then fill in the blanks.

22. Be true to your word and pay what you .... (Luke 12:58–59; 20:25; Romans 13:7)

23. Remember that "the borrower is .... to the lender" (Proverbs 22:7). This means that when you borrow, you are at the mercy of the lender. You are not usually in a position to control the terms of the agreement.

‹ Discussing and Pondering ›

‹ Preparing for Tough Times ›

In the USA, we are used to a high standard of living, and it is easy to feel that we have a right to the blessings we enjoy. But really, no one has a right to the "American Dream." The story of Joseph should warn us that prosperity comes from the Lord, and He can take it away if He chooses[17] (Job 1:21).

We must "store up" and prepare for times of trials and hardship. Persecution is the normal experience of those who follow Christ, and present peace should not lull us into carelessness. Economic and social stability are fragile and can end without warning, so it is ignorant and foolish to coast through life without preparing for change. As freedoms erode, we face the real possibility of persecution if we stand with Jesus. How can we prepare? What matters are worthy of our focus? Should we invest in gold, real estate, food, or seeds? Who or what can we rely on in bad times?

List some ways we should store up for an uncertain future.

1. ....
2. ....
3. ....

Read Matthew 6:24–34 and try to summarize its message in a sentence or two.

4. ....

‹ You Are a Steward ›

Read Luke 12:41–47 and Deuteronomy 8:17–18; then write your thoughts on the following questions.

5. What has God entrusted you with?

....
....

6. What does God want you to do with His possessions?

   ....
   ....
   ....

7. How will you give account of your managing?

   ....
   ....
   ....

8. Whose money do you really handle—yours or God's? ....

‹ Planning to Share ›

When Joseph stored grain, he was not hoarding it for himself, but saving it for others. It is also important to note that he was storing up for a known purpose—not as insurance against unknown calamities.

Times of prosperity are not given to make us complacent and lazy. God has placed us where we are, with our resources and abilities, to give us the opportunity to share with others. Do not wait to share until you have a lot to give. "Giving isn't a luxury of the rich. It's a privilege of the poor."[18]

‹ Thoughts to Ponder ›

Read the following passages and think about or discuss the questions.
- Deuteronomy 8:10–14 – Do you tend to forget God in times of prosperity?
- Ephesians 4:28 – What is the purpose of honest work?
- Proverbs 11:24–26 – Can a stingy person expect blessings?
- 2 Corinthians 8:2–5 – Is a poor person disqualified from giving?
- 2 Corinthians 9:6 – How will a generous person reap?
- Proverbs 14:31 and 17:5 – Who is mocked when we despise the poor?
- Proverbs 22:9 – Do you have a bountiful eye?
- James 1:27 – What does God say is pure religion?
- James 2:15–16 – Do you agree that words are cheap?
- Acts 20:35 – What is better than receiving?

‹ A Handout or a Hand Up ›

In light of what the Scriptures teach about giving, why didn't Joseph just give away the stored grain during the famine instead of selling it? One possible reason is that giving people money or goods outright is not always the best way to help them. Often it is better if people work for what they are given.

Giving handouts is not always best for the giver either. Simply giving something can serve to salve our conscience and free us from a sense of further responsibility for those in need.

9. **Review the story of Joseph's food distribution and see if you can come up with some reasons why Joseph may have required the people to buy their food.**

....
....
....
....

‹ Word Search: Riches ›

The puzzle below contains words representing things that can become false sources of security or happiness. The earthly things people heap up for themselves are temporary and unsatisfying; they will all fail us in the end.

Find all the words from the list below the puzzle, striking them through as you locate them. When you are finished marking all the words, you will find that the unused letters spell an important message from God.

B	D	O	S	T	E	K	N	I	R	T	W	D	L	O	G
O	S	N	T	F	I	N	E	D	I	N	I	N	G	T	R
O	E	T	E	L	E	V	I	S	I	O	N	U	M	E	S
K	E	N	O	I	H	S	A	F	T	I	E	N	U	N	S
S	R	U	N	M	A	K	E	U	P	C	E	B	S	I	E
R	G	N	I	P	A	C	S	D	N	A	L	O	I	C	U
C	E	T	J	O	B	N	I	A	V	R	I	A	C	I	Q
E	D	N	R	I	I	O	C	S	A	E	C	T	C	D	I
L	S	F	H	S	K	I	R	H	C	T	D	S	L	E	T
L	R	R	C	T	E	T	E	O	A	I	N	E	O	M	N
P	A	I	A	E	S	A	X	E	T	R	A	S	T	E	A
H	C	E	M	R	L	E	E	S	I	E	L	U	H	S	G
O	D	N	P	E	O	R	F	T	O	M	I	O	I	U	R
N	O	D	E	O	O	C	S	E	N	E	T	H	N	T	I
E	O	S	R	M	T	E	O	P	S	N	T	S	G	H	Y
6	F	:	S	1	7	R	S	R	E	T	U	P	M	O	C

Antiques	Cell phone	Fine dining	Job	Pets	Tools
Bikes	Clothing	Food	Land	Recreation	Trinkets
Boats	Computers	Friends	Landscaping	Retirement	Vacations
Books	Degrees	Gold	Makeup	Shoes	Wine
Campers	Exercise	Guns	Medicine	Stereo	
Cars	Fashion	Houses	Music	Television	

Engaging Yourself—Memorization and Application

1 Peter 5:7
Repeating a verse as you memorize helps you become familiar with it. Emphasizing a different word each time you repeat a passage can help impress its practical meaning on your heart as you emphasize different aspects of the truth. For example, you could read 1 Peter 5:7 like this:

- ***Casting*** all your care upon Him; for He careth for you.
- Casting ***all*** your care upon Him . . .
- Casting all ***your*** care upon Him . . .

How Rich Are You?
According to the 2014 poverty guidelines in the continental Unites States, a person who makes $11,670 or less annually is considered below the poverty level. However on the global scale, someone who makes this much is among the top 15% of the world's rich.

Write your thoughts.

1. List some of the forms of wealth God has given you.

   ....
   ....
   ....

2. What are some specific things you should be saving for the future? What are your goals for accomplishing this?

   ....
   ....
   ....
   ....

‹ Quiz 7 ›

Answer *True* or *False*.

1. Joseph began to store up grain three years before the famine came. ....

2. You are definitely holy if you are poor. ....

3. Sharing possessions is something only the rich can do. ....

Fill in the blank.

4. Jesus told a story of a rich man who was a .... because he laid up treasure for himself.

Write the correct answer.

5. What kind of treasure did Jesus say we should *not* lay up?
   ....

6. What should we be preparing for?
   ....

7. If your treasure and your heart were a truck and trailer, which would come first?
   ....

8. Why has God given us possessions and the ability to gain wealth?
   ....

9. What three things cannot happen to a Christian's inheritance in heaven?
   ....
   ....
   ....

10. Write 1 Peter 5:7 from memory.

   ....
   ....
   ....
   ....
   ....

LESSON 6

Success and Responsibility

Our character is not only tested during pressure and trials, but also during blessing and promotion. It is possible to stay grounded in God through trials, only to fizzle out when our lives begin to go more smoothly. Our true character is revealed by both the heat of the sun and the dew of blessings. We can grow through times of need and times of plenty, and God's school of life will take us through both.

We know how Joseph handled pressure, pits, and prison. How did he do with power and responsibility? How did he treat those under him?

Joseph began by being faithful in small things, seeking to please God in every task he did, and when he was blessed, he did not forget God. Power and fame did not go to his head because he recognized that his gifts and talents were given him by God, to be used under God's direction.

Like Joseph, we are called to be faithful, both when our efforts are unnoticed and when they bring us honor and recognition.

EXERCISES

Analyzing God's Word

Some people have suggested that Joseph must have flaunted his fine coat and his startling dreams to his brothers. If he did, he must have learned from it, for we do not see Joseph acting in pride or lording it over others again.

Read the passages below and answer the questions.

Genesis 39:1–6

1. Do you think Joseph's good looks went to his head? ....

2. How did people know the Lord was blessing Joseph? Did he have to tell others that God was with him?
....
....

3. To whom did Joseph credit his success? ....

4. Why do people like to be near someone God is blessing?

....

5. How much did Potiphar trust Joseph? ....

Genesis 39:21–23

6. Who favored Joseph in prison? ....

7. Who was responsible for all that happened in the prison? ....

8. Did Joseph ever rebel or start an uprising, either in prison or in Potiphar's house? ....

Genesis 41

9. According to the butler, Joseph was the servant of whom? ....

10. What did Joseph say about his reputation for interpreting dreams?

....

11. After Joseph interpreted Pharaoh's dreams, he offered Pharaoh a suggestion. Who would benefit if Pharaoh followed Joseph's advice?

....

12. Did Joseph try to get retribution for all he had suffered? ....

Genesis 47:13–26

13. Did Joseph have compassion on others who were suffering? ....

14. What was the attitude of the people of Egypt toward Joseph? ....

‹ Building Your Word Knowledge ›

‹ What Is Success? ›

Success is the accomplishment of a goal, the reaching of a prize.

1. In your words, define a successful person. How much money must he or she have? What kind of title would such a person have? How many people take orders from this person?

....

....

2. How far should a person be willing to go to be successful?

....

....

Read Matthew 6:21–23 and 16:26; then answer the following questions.

3. What goal are you striving for in your life? ....

4. Is your goal worthy of the effort you are giving it? ....

5. Who has set this goal for you? ....

6. What will your reward be if you are successful in reaching your goal?
....
....

‹ What Is Leadership? ›

A leader is someone who guides by setting the direction, going in advance, or setting the example.

7. It seems nearly everyone wants to be a leader. But how do you get there? Do you just wake up one morning as the one in charge?
....
....

8. A good leader is someone who has first learned to follow. Think of a leader, boss, parent, or teacher whom you admire. How did he or she come to this position?
....
....

9. What characteristics do you admire in those you consider successful?
....
....

> "Seest thou a man diligent in his business? he shall stand before kings; he shall not stand before mean men" (Proverbs. 22:29).

‹ Qualities of Good Leaders ›

In each question below, circle the italicized word or phrase that describes a quality of good leaders.

10. Are good leaders *gentle* or *intimidating*?
11. Are they *hard-nosed* or *flexible*?
12. Do they *lack concern* for others or *decide with fairness*?
13. Are they *wasteful* or *careful* with their possessions?
14. What is more important to them, *people* or *property*?
15. Are they *willing to get dirty* or are they *above menial tasks*?
16. Do they *hold others down* or do they *encourage creativity*?

72   Integrity: A study on the life of Joseph

17. Are they *orderly* or *sloppy?*

18. Are they *accountable* to others or are they *untouchable?* (Colossians 4:1)

19. Are they *humble* or *proud* of their accomplishments?

20. Do they *resist* correction or *accept* it with grace?

In Luke 16:10, Jesus said, "He that is faithful in that which is least is faithful also in much." We can predict what kind of leader a person would be by observing how he or she handles small responsibilities. Jesus said, "Blessed are the merciful . . ." (Matthew 5:7), and "It is more blessed to give than to receive" (Acts 20:35). Have you found the freedom that comes from serving others?

Even humiliating experiences can teach us faithfulness. While Silvia Tarniceriu and Elena Boghian were in a Romanian prison camp because of their faith in Christ, they were told to clean out a cell full of human excrement with their bare hands. Then they were forced to go to dinner without soap or warm water to wash with. God protected them and enabled them to do this disgusting task for Him. [14]

He who is too proud to bow is too weak to lead.

‹ Leaders in the Bible ›

See how many of the following questions you can answer.

21. Who organized the building of a city wall that took only fifty-two days? ....

22. Who made a league of peace with the Gibeonites without first inquiring of God? ....

23. Which leader sent 99% of his army home because God said he had too many men to win the battle?
....

24. Who had compassion when he saw the multitudes? ....

25. Which leader said, "I will not offer a sacrifice that cost me nothing"? ....

26. Which leader was said to be the meekest man on the earth? ....

27. Which king was struck with leprosy because he was lifted up in pride and tried to offer incense in the temple?
....

28. Which king began a national revival of faith in God at the age of sixteen and found the book of the Law hidden in the temple?
....

29. Which king pouted when he couldn't get his way, allowed his wife to run the kingdom, and killed an innocent man?
....

30. Who said, "Be ye followers of me, even as I also am of Christ"? ....

Comparing Scripture with Scripture

Are You Ready to Lead?

Joseph may have considered himself mature and ready to tackle great things at seventeen years old, but although his father gave him large responsibilities while he was young, God did not consider Joseph ready to be a ruler. He needed slavery and prison to purify and polish him, teaching him the vital lessons he would need to be a great leader. Only God knows when we are ready for leadership. When God gives us a dream, it usually takes time for it to materialize.

Circle the correct number to complete each sentence.

1. Joseph was .... years old when he became ruler of Egypt (Genesis 41:46).

    30   40   60

2. Although anointed as a boy, David did not receive the kingdom until age .... (2 Samuel 5:4).

    20   30   40

3. Moses felt ready to lead at 40, but God made him wait another .... years (Exodus 7:7).

    10   20   40

4. Abraham was .... when his promised son was born (Genesis 21:5).

    40   50   100

5. Jesus did not begin His ministry until He was .... (Luke 3:23).

    30   40   50

"Wait on the LORD: be of good courage, and he shall strengthen thine heart: wait, I say, on the LORD" (Psalm 27:14). While you wait, stay busy doing the small tasks you are given. The small duties of today are building blocks for tomorrow. Our focus will be changed and our authorities will be blessed when we realize that we are really serving Jesus (Ephesians 6:5–7).

No matter where we serve, God is our ultimate Master. Our decisions should not be affected by who is watching us, for we are to live not for the praise of people, but with the sole purpose of pleasing God in all we do. Making the "Audience of One" our goal will bring us purpose and joy[15] (Colossians 3:22–24).

Success with God

Look up the references to complete the sentences.

6. "................... yourselves therefore under the mighty hand of God, that he may exalt you in due time" (1 Peter 5:6).

7. Above all else, Paul wanted Christ to be magnified in his body. He boldly declared, "For to me to live is .... , and to .... is gain" (Philippians 1:20–21).

8. We will be rewarded at the proper time if we do not .... (Galatians 6:9).

9. An evil heart of .... will keep you from God's success (Hebrews 3:12; 18–19).

10. We must .... if we want to enter into God's rest (Hebrews 4:11).

11. The .... will not succeed (Proverbs 6:9–11).

12. The Apostle Paul said in Philippians 4:11–12 that he knew both how to be abased, and how to .... He had learned both to be .... and to be hungry, both to .... and to suffer need.

Look up the references to answer the questions.

13. According to Joshua 1:8, what is God's secret for success?

....
....
....

14. According to Philippians 3:8–14, what things did the Apostle Paul value? What prize was he striving for?

....
....
....

‹ Good Worker Checklist ›

- ☐ Do you keep a promise even if it hurts? (Psalm 15:4)
- ☐ Are you known to be lazy? (Proverbs 10:26)
- ☐ Are you wasteful? (Luke 15:13)
- ☐ Are you trustworthy? Do you take responsibility for the results of your work?
- ☐ Are you willing to learn?
- ☐ Do you respect others' tools, time, and reputations?
- ☐ Do you encourage dissatisfaction among other workers by complaining?
- ☐ Do you talk back to or contradict those in authority over you? (Titus 2:9)

‹ Discussing and Pondering ›

Write your thoughts.

1. Should the pursuit of wealth and status be the goal of your life? Are you willing to trample others to reach your goals?

....

2. How far will you go to get a good deal? Are you so "frugal" that you drag the name of Christ through the dirt by taking advantage of the generosity or ignorance of others?

....

3. What would you do if you bought a house and then found $45,000 in the attic (this has actually happened)? Would you consider it a windfall for yourself, or would you try to find out who lost it?

4. What would you do if you found a car for sale dirt-cheap because of a bitter divorce settlement, and you knew it was worth a lot more?

5. If God has given you strength, talents, intelligence, money, health, a home, or an opportunity to live in a prosperous nation, what do you think His purpose is? Are these things for you to spend on yourself and to use to keep others in their places?

6. If you gain an honored position, greater status, or a high income, how do you think you will be affected? Will the increased power corrupt you?

7. Do you feel you deserve wealth, status, and fame, or do you consider it an unearned responsibility entrusted to you by God? (Consider Joseph's attitude in Genesis 39:9.)

8. Is it important to you that others recognize your accomplishments?

9. Covetousness is a form of idolatry. How can you protect yourself from being consumed by the love of riches? How do you keep your possessions as servants instead of masters?

10. Do you handle both large and small assets as a steward for God? (Colossians 3:23)

11. Do you have a character God can safely entrust with greater responsibility?

12. As a slave, Joseph showed loyalty and responsibility toward his master. Would it have been okay for Joseph to steal from or sabotage Potiphar's house in an effort to even the score? (See 1 Timothy 6:1 and Titus 2:9)

13. Do you feel as if you deserve to take from those in authority over you or give them half-hearted work, since they have more than they need anyway?

   ....

Joseph sought to bless and prosper those he served. Like Joseph, we find success by working for the success of those to whom we are responsible (see Philippians 2:4).

‹ Engaging Yourself—Memorization and Application ›

‹ Colossians 3:17 ›

1. **Memorize Colossians 3:17 and write it below.**

   ....
   ....
   ....
   ....
   ....

Write your thoughts.

2. If you were a boss looking to hire a new employee, what qualities would you look for?

   ....
   ....

3. What are some responsibilities you already have that you should commit to do better at?

   ....
   ....

4. What are some work habits you can cultivate now that will help you be more successful?

   ....
   ....

5. Read 1 Corinthians 10:31–33 and make a list of the people you are called to serve.

   ....
   ....

6. What are some personal resources, talents, and skills you have that you can use for the glory of God? How can you use them to bless others around you?

   ....
   ....

‹ Quiz 6 ›

Answer *True* or *False*.

1. Joseph told Pharaoh his boyhood dream about sheaves bowing down to him. ....

2. Joseph was thirty years old when he was made ruler of Egypt. ....

Fill in the blanks.

3. A good leader is someone who has first learned to ....

4. People recognized that Joseph had the Spirit of God. Pharaoh said of him, "There is none so .... and .... as thou art" (Genesis 41:39).

5. The Apostle Paul learned to be content in all situations. This included times of adversity and times of ....

Answer the questions.

6. Did Joseph see his promotion as *something he deserved* for the injustice he had suffered, or as an *opportunity and responsibility* to save people's lives?
   ....

7. What is the meaning of "living for the Audience of One"?
   ....

8. Is a leader someone who *tells others what to do* or someone who *guides by setting an example*?
   ....

9. What should we meditate on if we want to succeed?
   ....

10. Write Colossians 3:17 from memory.

....

....

....

....

....

LESSON 8

Joseph Tests His Brothers

When Joseph's brothers came to Egypt to buy grain, he was thirty-seven years old and had not seen them in over twenty years. A lot can happen in twenty years. A childhood acquaintance who was annoying and overbearing may have grown into a generous employer or a preacher. Someone you used to look up to may have made a series of bad choices and become a hardened cynic.

We don't want others to try to lock us in our past, yet it's easy for us to do that to them. Although we know the potential for change, when we encounter people we knew long ago, we tend to imagine them as we last knew them.

Joseph knew God can change hearts over time, but he did not know what kind of men his brothers had become. To see how they had changed, he tested them.

Students often dread taking tests, but they are necessary to measure growth. Tests can tell us how far we have come and how much we know. Tests in our lives reveal whether we have learned the lessons God is teaching us, and when we are ready for more responsibility.

The tests Joseph gave his brothers forced them to face their past and allowed them to move on. Without Joseph's examination, his brothers may have spent the rest of their lives in hidden sorrow and shame. It must have been embarrassing to tell their father what they had really done more than twenty years before. But, oh, the freedom they gained! Indeed, as Jesus said, "The truth shall make you free" (John 8:32).

EXERCISES

‹ Analyzing God's Word ›

Read Genesis 42–44; then answer the questions and fill in the blanks.

1. What did Joseph's ten brothers do when they came before the governor to buy grain?

   ....

2. What was the name of the great governor who had predicted the famine and now held all sustenance in his power?

   ....

3. What did the governor accuse Joseph's brothers of? ....

4. Did he know who they were? ....

5. Why did Joseph keep his identity secret?
....

6. Why do you think he threw his brothers into prison? Was he getting even?
....

7. What did Joseph require his brothers to do to verify the story they told him about their family?
....

8. Why did Joseph's brothers think this trouble had come upon them?
....

9. What did Joseph do that frightened his brothers on the way home?
....

10. How did Joseph test his brothers' honesty?
....

11. Did Jacob trust Reuben to be responsible for Benjamin? ....

12. Who persuaded Jacob to let his youngest son go? ....

13. What did the brothers take with them on the second trip to gain favor with the governor?
....

14. The second time Joseph's brothers visited, he treated them as honored guests but gave five times as much food to ....

15. To see if his brothers were looking for an opportunity to get rid of their father's favorite son, Benjamin, Joseph accused Benjamin of what?
....

16. What did Joseph demand as a punishment for stealing the cup?
....

17. What did Judah offer Joseph in exchange for releasing Benjamin?
....

18. What did Joseph want his brothers to do after he told them who he was?
....

‹ Building Your Word Knowledge ›

‹ Testing ›

The word *test* is not found in the KJV Bible, but there are many words with the same meaning. In the following exercises you will explore what the Bible teaches about testing and its purposes.

Below are the *Strong's* numbers for some Hebrew and Greek words that refer to testing. Using a *Strong's Concordance*, look up each word; then write the word and definition on the line next to the number.

On the second line, list some references where the word is found.

(Refer to Lesson 4 if you need to refresh your memory on the use of *Strong's Concordance*. Remember to differentiate between the Hebrew OT and the Greek NT.)

1. 0974 ....
   Bible references: ....

2. 02713 ....
   Bible references: ....

3. 05254 ....
   Bible references: ....

4. 06884 ....
   Bible references: ....

5. 1381 ....
   Bible references: ....

6. 3985 ....
   Bible references: ....

Can you find other words related to testing that are not listed above? You may write the number, word, definition, and references in the spaces below.

7. ....
   ....

8. ....
   ....

9. ....
   ....

Integrity: A study on the life of Joseph

10. _____

Note: In Greek, letters added to the beginning and end of a word change the form and verb tense. There are also "morphs" that specify gender, parts of speech (noun, verb, etc.), number, and tense. Because of this, two seemingly different words may be forms of the same word. As you gain experience, you will learn to look for the main root that is common to such entries.

On the lines below, list the references of any verses from the exercise above that you have additional questions about.

11. _____

Write your thoughts.

12. How do you harmonize the account in Genesis 22, where God "tempted" Abraham, with James 1:13–14, which says God tempts no one?
    _____

13. If God sends a test, what is His purpose in it for you? _____

14. When Satan tests or tempts you, what is his purpose? _____

15. Can the context of a verse tell you if the word *tempt* means "test" or "entice"? _____

16. What does it mean to *prove* something?
    _____

17. When is it wrong to put God to the test?
    _____

18. Why might we test people? (John 6:6; 1 John 4:1)
    _____

‹ Comparing Scripture with Scripture ›

‹ Healing Relationships with Wisdom ›

"He that hath no rule over his own spirit is like a city that is broken down, and without walls" (Proverbs 25:28).

Marsyas

When Joseph encountered his brothers in Egypt, his actions showed maturity and self-control. He waited to judge them until he tested them to find out how they may have changed. When he learned that they were truly sorry for their wrongdoing and were seeking to change, he saw that it would be pointless to rebuke them for the past, and he never did.

There is a time and a place to reprove sin, but we need to discern the situation first, as Joseph did, and act with the good of the other person in mind.

Crossword Puzzle: Maturity in Relationships

The verses referenced in this crossword puzzle reveal the virtues that made Joseph who he was. They also give direction for dealing with difficult relationships in our own lives.

ACROSS

2. If you answer a matter before you hear it, it is a .... to you (Proverbs 18:13).
3. To disregard; loath (Proverbs 23:9)
6. We are not to give holy things to these creatures (Matthew 7:6).
8. "And of some have .... , making a difference" (Jude 1:22).
10. The strongest body part (Proverbs 21:23)
11. Charity (Proverbs 9:8)
12. "Answer .... a fool" (Proverbs 26:4).
13. A fool's way of life; rhymes with jolly (Proverbs 26:4)
16. Does not endure to every generation (Proverbs 27:24)
17. Something God hates (Proverbs 17:15)
20. Wringing this brings forth blood (Proverbs 30:33).
21. Sacred (Matthew 7:6)

22. "A .... name is rather to be chosen . . ." (Proverbs 22:1)
24. Opposite of go (Proverbs 6:12–15)
26. "A fool uttereth all ...." (Proverbs 29:11).
28. "................ a fool" (Proverbs 26:5).
30. "Doth our law .... any man?" (John 7:51)
32. Not fast (James 1:19)
34. Destitute (Proverbs 29:14)
35. Anger (James 1:19)
36. Opposite of foolish (Proverbs 14:15)

DOWN

1. Thoughts of our minds (Proverbs 6:18)
4. Of the highest quality (Proverbs 17:27)
5. Rhymes with *way* (Job 38:37)
7. Someone who says everything he thinks (Proverbs 29:11)
9. Harmless (Proverbs 6:16–17)

84   Integrity: A study on the life of Joseph

14. To forgive will bring you .... (Proverbs 19:11).
15. "He will despise the .... of thy words" (Proverbs 23:9).
18. "They be .... leaders of the ...." (Matthew 15:14).
19. Opposite of cruel (Proverbs 11:17)
21. Opposite of she (Proverbs 6:11–14)
23. Lack of harmony in relationships (Proverbs 6:19)
25. Myself (Proverbs 1:33)
27. ".................... not a scorner" (Proverbs 9:8).
28. If you are slow to experience this emotion, you are better than a strong person (Proverbs 16:32).
29. "Rebuke a .... man, and he will love thee" (Proverbs 9:8).
31. Fast (Proverbs 6:18)
33. "The .... of truth shall be established forever" (Proverbs 12:19).

‹ lesson 8 › Joseph Tests His Brothers 85

‹ Godly Sorrow ›

Write your thoughts.

1. How can you show that you are truly sorry for a wrong you have done?

   ....

   ....

Look up the references to find the answers.

2. What are we to do before we offer a gift or service to God? (Matthew 5:23–24)

   ....

3. In 2 Samuel 12:13, David confessed that he had really sinned against whom? ....
   (Also read Psalm 32:5 and 51:4.)

4. What are the results of godly sorrow versus worldly sorrow? (2 Corinthians 7:10)

   ....

   ....

5. What do Matthew 26:75 and Matthew 27:3–5 show us about the difference between godly and worldly sorrow?

   ....

   ....

‹ Repentance and Consequences ›

Write your thoughts.

6. Does asking for forgiveness erase the wrong one has done and return everything to the way it was before? .... Why or why not? ....

7. Are you living with the consequences of something you did in the past? If so, write what you did and the consequences you are living with today.

   ....

   ....

8. Can God bring beauty out of ashes? ....

9. Does God's ability to restore and heal excuse our wrongdoing? ....

10. Does God's forgiveness leave us free to continue in a sinful lifestyle? (Romans 5:20; 6:1–2) ....

11. What were Jesus' final words to the woman caught in adultery? (John 8:1–11)

    ....

    ....

12. Can we expect our broken relationships with others to be completely restored as soon as we are forgiven?

Discussing and Pondering

True Freedom and True Slavery

Write your thoughts.

1. Describe the worst kind of prison you can imagine.

2. Was Joseph bound by the wrongs others did to him?

3. Describe the guilt Joseph's brothers must have been carrying.

When Joseph's brothers arrived in Egypt, Joseph had spent more than half the previous twenty years as a slave or a prisoner in body. Yet he was not shackled by hate or bound by bitterness. His faith in God's goodness and sovereignty allowed him to live boldly and without fear.

In contrast, between the time Joseph's brothers sold him and when they met him in Egypt, they had never been slaves or prisoners—but were they free? Imagine the ever-present fear of their evil being found out and the constant worry about God's punishment. Imagine their pain as they watched their father grieve for the son he thought was dead. They must have often felt trapped, with no way of knowing where Joseph was and no way to atone for their sin.

Although his brothers had sold Joseph in order to forget his dreams and keep them from coming true, they succeeded in neither.

Who was really bound—Joseph or his brothers?

Some prisons have physical walls that obstruct our view, limit our movement, and separate us from others, but there are prisons of the mind and spirit which are just as real. Fear, hate, and bitterness are such prisons. Guilt robs us of the freedom to enjoy life. Grudges bind us to the past and damage us more than the person we seek to hurt. Secret sins lock us into a dark cell and eat away at us.

The most devastating of all prisons are those we choose ourselves.

JeanBono

Think about the following question and write your answer.

4. Are you locked in any invisible prisons? If so, what are they?

....

....

....

....

‹ Correcting and Confronting in Love ›

Underline the correct ending to each sentence.

5. In a way, Joseph was testing his brothers to
    a. make himself feel better.
    b. lead them toward restoration and healing.

6. Joseph's testing and words to his brothers helped them
    a. see their own sinfulness and break the chains of sin in which they lived.
    b. admire their own decision to sell him so he could help them now.

7. By the time Joseph's brothers were reunited with him, they had become
    a. angrier and more hateful.
    b. better in some ways.

8. Joseph's brothers had tried to reform their lives and do better, but they still were not
    a. free.
    b. hungry.

9. Joseph helped his brothers find freedom because of his
    a. forgiveness and love.
    b. hate and bitterness.

10. Joseph may have been concerned that his family might break up from bitterness and hatred, and that they would ultimately lose[19]
    a. the silver cup.
    b. God's promises to Abraham.

The Ever-Tightening Handcuff of Lies

Joseph's brothers were bound by handcuffs of their own making. Once you tell a lie, you can never forget it, because it will require other lies to keep it covered

Joseph's Compassionate Confrontation

Write your thoughts.

11. Did Joseph let his emotions control him when he confronted his brothers? ....

12. How did Joseph manage his emotions during his encounters with his brothers?

....

....

13. Did Joseph allow past hurts, anger, revenge, or the tension of the moment to make him do something he would regret? ....

Just the Way We Are

Write your thoughts.

14. People often say, "God loves us just the way we are!" In your own words, what do you think people usually mean by this? ....

15. Is it true that God loves us just as we are? ....

16. Is God willing to let us stay "just the way we are"? ....

God's whole plan of redemption involves redeeming us from ourselves—taking us from where we are to where He wants us to be. This is the work of God's transforming love.

Are we like this? Do we love everyone—even our bitterest enemies—enough to not merely ignore them, but to help them reach their full potential? Do we seek healing and restoration, even for those who have hurt us?

When we overlook sin or "sweep it under the carpet" in the name of being gracious and forgiving, we can unwittingly do people a great disservice. Christian communities and individuals who fail to hold people accountable for their wrongdoing can send the message that sin is no big deal, causing much harm to those ensnared by it.

‹ Purposes for Punishment ›

Answer the question and complete the Scripture quotes.

17. According to 2 Samuel 12:14, what opportunity did David's sin provide to the enemies of God?
....

18. Hebrews 12:11 says, "Now no chastening for the present seemeth to be joyous, but grievous: nevertheless afterward it yieldeth the .... unto them which are exercised thereby."

19. Left unchecked, sin will become a stronghold in people's lives. "Because sentence against an evil work is not executed .... , therefore the heart of the sons of men is .... in them to do evil" (Ecclesiastes 8:11).

Engaging Yourself—Memorization and Application

Proverbs 27:6

Write your thoughts.

1. Are there things you have done that God is asking you to make right? If so, name them.

   ....
   ....
   ....
   ....

2. Is there a person or situation you need to care enough about to address or confront? Who or what?

   ....

3. What are some precautions you could take to avoid doing or saying something rash when you confront someone?

   ....
   ....
   ....

4. **Memorize Proverbs 27:6; then use the lines below to write its meaning in your own words.**

   ....
   ....
   ....
   ....
   ....

‹ Quiz 8 ›

Answer *True* or *False*.

1. Joseph immediately recognized his brothers, but they did not recognize him. ....

2. Jacob sent his sons to Egypt to find Joseph. ....

3. Overlooking sin helps people because it makes them comfortable. ....

Answer the questions.

4. Joseph's brothers may have hoped that by selling Joseph they could forget about him. What did they say that showed they had not been able to forget?
   ....

5. How many years passed from the time Joseph's brothers sold him until they saw him again? ....

6. Name three tests Joseph gave his brothers:
   a. ....
   b. ....
   c. ....

7. Which brother offered to serve as a slave in Benjamin's place? ....

Fill in the blanks.

8. Joseph made himself .... to his brothers by speaking roughly through an interpreter.

9. If judgment against sin is not executed speedily, people may find their heart .... to do evil.

10. **Write Proverbs 27:6 from memory.**

    ....
    ....
    ....
    ....
    ....

‹ lesson 8 › Joseph Tests His Brothers

LESSON 9

Revenge or Forgiveness?

The Scriptures say that when Joseph revealed himself to his brothers, "they were troubled at his presence" (Genesis 45:3).

Their minds must have been filled with remorse for all the evil they had done to Joseph. They realized that in bowing before him, they had fulfilled his dreams of long ago. However, their strongest emotion was probably fear—fear that Joseph would now seize his opportunity to take revenge. They were completely unprepared for what happened next!

EXERCISES

Analyzing God's Word

Read each passage below and answer the questions or fill in the blanks in the exercises that follow.

Genesis 45

1. Did Joseph consider himself too important to cry? ....

2. Was Joseph embarrassed to show his emotions? ....

3. Although Joseph's brothers had never revealed the identity of their missing brother to the governor, he spoke to them in their own .... saying, "I am Joseph your brother, whom ye .... into Egypt" (Genesis 45:4).

4. Joseph's brothers probably expected him to ....

5. Who did Joseph say was responsible for sending him into Egypt? ....

6. How could Joseph forgive and love his brothers in spite of all they had done to him?
....
....

7. How many more years of famine would there be? ....

8. To whom did Joseph say he had been made a father? ....

9. What land did Joseph want to give his family? ....

10. Joseph gave changes of clothes to all his brothers, but he gave ....
   .... to Benjamin.

11. What special instruction did Joseph give his brothers for the trip home?
   ....

Genesis 46:1–7, 27–34

12. God told Jacob, " .... to go down into Egypt. I will go down with thee into Egypt; and I will also surely bring thee ....: and Joseph shall put his hand upon thine eyes" (Genesis 46:4).

13. What did Joseph advise his family to tell Pharaoh about their occupation, and why?
   ....
   ....
   ....

Genesis 47:27–31

14. How many years did Jacob end up living in Egypt? ....

15. Where did Jacob want to be buried? ....

Genesis 49:22–26

16. Jacob blessed each of his sons before he died. Of Joseph, he said, "The archers have sorely grieved him, and .... at him, and .... him: but his bow abode in strength, and the arms of his hands were made strong by the hands of the .... " (Genesis 49:23–24).

Genesis 50

17. Where did the family of Joseph choose to live following the burial of their father? ....

18. After Jacob died, what did Joseph's brothers fear? ....

19. Joseph's brothers bowed before him again after Jacob's death and said, "Behold, we be thy
   .... " (Genesis 50:18).

20. Joseph said, "Fear not: for am I in the place of .... ?" (Genesis 50:19)

21. What good purpose of God did Joseph recognize?
....
....

22. Before he died at 110 years old, Joseph made his family promise to do what?
....

‹ Building Your Word Knowledge ›

‹ Forgiving Offenses and Enemies ›

Locating Scriptures by Word or Phrase

Sometimes you may remember a word or phrase from a verse, but not the reference where it is found. By looking up a keyword, you can use *Strong's Concordance* to locate the reference you want. Using an uncommon keyword or multiple keywords helps narrow down the list of references you will have to wade through. (Keep in mind that *Strong's* uses the spellings of the KJV, such as *saviour* and *neighbour*.)

Before doing the following exercises, look up the emphasized words below in an ordinary dictionary and write their definitions in the blanks.

1. To *forgive* means ....

2. An *offense* is ....

3. An *enemy* is ....

For each item, locate a verse that contains all the listed words; then write the reference in the blank (you need a software version of *Strong's* or the Bible for this).

4. offend, little, ones ....

5. offend, in, word ....

Locate the verse that contains the following phrase and write the reference in the blank.

6. "It is impossible but that offences will come." ....

Answer the following questions, using *Strong's Concordance* where necessary.

7. How many times does the word *forgive* occur in the KJV New Testament? ....

8. How many times are we to forgive someone? ....

9. What happens if we do not forgive others their trespasses?
....

10. To whom was Jesus referring when He said, "Father, forgive them; for they know not what they do"?

....

11. Who is the *he* referred to by the words, "If he hath wronged thee . . . put that on mine account"?

....

12. How often does the phrase "love thy neighbour" occur in the KJV Bible? ....

13. Jesus said to love your neighbor as yourself. But one man, seeking to justify himself, asked "Who is my neighbour?" How did Jesus answer?

....

....

....

14. What does the book of Proverbs say about how to treat our enemies?

....

Timely Forgiveness

A practical way to keep bitterness from taking root in our lives is to learn to forgive quickly. The practice of prompt forgiveness is like greasing your hands with butter to prevent dough from sticking to them when you are making bread, or like a duck that oils its feathers to keep water from soaking in. If we quickly and constantly release our hurts to God, they cannot stick to us or soak deeper.

We must choose not to be easily offended. Forgiveness is easiest if we let go of hurts right away and place them into God's capable hands where they belong.

We will find peace when we understand that everything that comes into our lives—even the cruelty of others—is part of God's plan to mold our lives for good.

‹ Comparing Scripture with Scripture ›

‹ The Destructive Logic of Revenge ›

When people seek revenge, they are not trying to get even—they are usually trying to get *ahead*. Revenge is about giving the other person as much pain as they caused me, plus some more on top. Retaliation always escalates like this.

In the Old Testament, God limited punishments to an eye for an eye and a tooth for a tooth—no more. Judgment was to be fair and even. Leviticus 24:17–22 and Deuteronomy 19:17–21 both give examples of the penalties God required of Old Testament Israel.

Leviticus 19:18 commanded the Hebrews to love their neighbors, but their religious teachers applied this command only to one's own family, friends, or nation. They considered their enemies outside the scope of this command (Matthew 5:43).

In the New Testament, Jesus calls His followers to live above the letter of the old law. When we are wronged, we are not to seek retribution but rather allow ourselves to be taken advantage of. We are to go beyond the call of duty, showing active love to those who mistreat us.

Read Matthew 5:38–48; then complete the Scripture quotes showing how God wants His children to live today.

1. "But I say unto you, That ye resist .... evil."

2. "But I say unto you, ... your enemies, bless them that .... you, do .... to them that hate you, and pray for them which despitefully .... you, and persecute you."

3. "For if ye love them which love you, what .... have ye?"

4. "Be ye therefore perfect, even as your .... which is in heaven is perfect."

Review the parable of the Good Samaritan (Luke 10:27–37) and answer the question.

5. According to Jesus, who is your neighbor? ....

Read the listed passages and fill in the blanks.

6. Romans 12:14, 17–21 – "Overcome evil with ...."

7. 1 Corinthians 6:7 – "Why do ye not rather take ....? Why do ye not rather suffer yourselves to be ....?"

8. 1 Peter 2:19–23 – "When ye do well, and suffer for it, ye take it patiently, this is .... with God. . . . Christ also suffered for us, leaving us an example, that ye should .... his steps: . . . when he suffered, he threatened not; but .... himself to him that judgeth righteously."

Read Mark 12:30–31 to answer the question.

9. What two commands sum up all the laws of God?

   a. ....
   b. ....

Match the first half of each verse to the second half.

10. Rejoice not when thine enemy falleth, ...

11. "Say not, I will do so to him as he hath done to me: ...."

12. "Hatred stirreth up strifes: ...."

13. "He that loveth his brother abideth in the light, ..."

a. But love covereth all sins" (Proverbs 10:12).

b. and let not thine heart be glad when he stumbleth" (Proverbs 24:17).

c. and there is none occasion of stumbling in him" (1 John 2:10).

d. I will render to the man according to his work" (Proverbs 24:29).

Unscramble two truths Joseph learned.

14. "Os won it saw ton oyu hatt tens em hihert, tub dog" (Genesis 45:8).

....

15. "Ye tgouhht live gainsat me; tbu odg teamn ti tonu godo" (Genesis 50:20).

....

‹ Discussing and Pondering ›

‹ How Do We Love Our Enemies? ›

Read 1 Corinthians 13:4–7 (if you are in a group, read the passage aloud as a responsive reading). Then write your thoughts on the following questions.

1. What does love look like in everyday attitudes?

....
....
....
....

2. Jesus made it clear that loving our enemies means more than merely refraining from retaliation. Love involves positive actions of goodwill toward those who hurt us. Can you think of a way you could show active love to someone who has hurt you?

....
....
....
....

‹ Forgiveness or Forgetfulness? ›

Forgiveness does not mean forgetting that a wrong ever happened. It means choosing to free the wrongdoer—to give up your demand for compensation. Forgiveness means letting go of all grudges, however justified they feel, even though the memory of the hurt may never be erased. In forgiveness, you release your hurts to God, choosing not to keep a list of wrongs (1 Peter 4:19).

It is sobering to realize that God will not forgive you if you refuse to forgive another person (Matthew 6:14–15). Someone has said, "Those who refuse to forgive destroy the very bridge over which they must cross."

Matthew 18:32–35 suggests that even things in your past can be brought up again and held against you if you refuse to forgive. Someone else's self-centeredness may have hurt you, but it is your own self-centeredness that keeps that hurt alive.

Write your thoughts.

3. What are some ways forgiveness benefits you?

   ....
   ....
   ....

4. Who else does forgiveness benefit? ....

5. How will refusing to forgive harm you?

   ....
   ....

6. Whose responsibility is it to "even the score"? ....

‹ Questions to Ponder ›

- How do you respond to adversity?
- How well do you handle criticism, slander, or cruelty?
- Are you quick to take up a grudge and slow to lay it down?
- Do you hold grudges over wrongs done to others?
- Do you aim for revenge, to just get even, or to do good in exchange for the evil done to you?
- Would you sue others for damages if they harmed you?
- Can you place your life in the hands of the perfect Judge and trust Him to bring justice, or do you fear that the person who hurt you will "get away with it"?

"Say not thou, I will recompense evil; but wait on the LORD, and he shall save thee" (Proverbs 20:22).

‹ Engaging Yourself—Memorization and Application ›

‹ Matthew 5:44 ›

1. **Write Matthew 5:44 on the lines below.**

   ....
   ....
   ....
   ....

Complete the following exercises on the memory verse you wrote above.

2. Above the pronoun *I*, write the name of the person speaking.

3. Circle the four action verbs—things we are to do.

4. Underline the descriptions of the people whom we are to treat this way.

5. Draw a box around the twelve-letter adverb that describes how people may treat you.

6. Quote Matthew 5:44 to someone and pray that God will enable you to live it out.

Do you think people who treat you as the memory verse describes deserve your love? Do you deserve God's love? True forgiveness is love for the undeserving. Only as you have accepted God's love will you be able to give it to others.

Read 1 John 3:11–18 and 1 John 4:7–8, 11, 19–21.

Write your thoughts.

7. Think of someone who is your enemy—or even someone you don't consider an enemy, but whom you just don't like. What would God want you to do for that person?

   ....
   ....

8. List some blessings you can pray for on behalf of those who have mistreated you.

   ....
   ....
   ....
   ....
   ....
   ....

‹ Quiz 9 ›

Answer *True* or *False*.

1. Joseph said, "It was not you that sent me hither, but Satan." ....

2. Jesus said there is nothing remarkable about loving those who love you. ....

Answer the questions.

3. How did the governor of Egypt know what Israel's sons had done to their brother Joseph?
   ....

4. In what part of Egypt did Joseph's family settle?
   ....

5. What happens if we do not forgive men their trespasses?
   ....

6. Who is harmed most when we are bitter and unforgiving?
   ....

7. With what are we to overcome evil? ....

8. According to Jesus, how many times are we to forgive someone? ....

9. To whom should we commit the keeping of our souls—the responsibility to protect us and carry out justice when others wrong us?
   ....

10. Write Matthew 5:44 from memory.

....

....

....

....

....

LESSON 10
Jesus—Deliverer for Mankind

The entrance of sin into the world destroyed mankind's relationship with God, and humanity was cursed with separation and death. However, this tragedy did not catch God by surprise; He has always had a plan to defeat sin and redeem humanity. The entire Bible describes the development of God's plan of redemption. All throughout the Old Testament, God supplied symbols, hints, and prophecies to His people that someday the curse would be broken.

God said in the Old Testament that the life is in the blood (Leviticus 17:11). The shedding of blood in the Old Testament sacrificial system represented one life being exchanged for another. This was one of many illustrations God provided to show us that He would bring Someone to die in our place and restore our broken relationship with Him. Many people died before the Deliverer came. However, God accepted and forgave those who obeyed the revelation they had and set their hopes on the coming Saviour. They looked forward to the sacrifice of Jesus, and we look back to it. The only hope for them and us is to trust in God's salvation.

God has said that the soul that sins shall die. But in Christ, God took our place and died for us. Only one who was perfect could do this. Christ could not have delivered us from sin had He needed deliverance Himself.

God's plan of salvation is the theme of the Bible. The development of this plan throughout history has been called *The Red Ribbon of His-Story*.

EXERCISES

◂ Analyzing God's Word ▸

Pictures of Redemption

Read the references below. For each reference or set of references, find the Old Testament illustration of God's plan of salvation through Jesus.

1. Genesis 3:15; John 12:30–32 ....

2. Genesis 3:21 ....

3. Genesis 4:4 ....

4. Genesis 6:11–19 ....

5. Genesis 22:7–14 ....

6. Genesis 22:18; Galatians 3:16 ....

7. Exodus 12:3–13 ....

8. Exodus 17:5–7; John 7:38; 1 Corinthians 10:4 ....

9. Leviticus 4:29–31; John 1:29; Hebrews 9:1–12 ....

10. Numbers 21:6–9; John 3:14–15 ....

11. Ruth 3:8–13; 4:14–15 ....

12. 2 Samuel 7:12–16; Luke 1:32 ....

13. Isaiah 53; Matthew 27 ....

14. Psalm 16:10; Acts 13:33–37; Matthew 28:5–6 ....

Read 1 Corinthians 2:7–9 and Ephesians 3:8–11; then write your thoughts on the question below.

15. Why did God wrap His plan of redemption in mystery? Why was it hidden throughout the Old Testament?

....

....

....

‹ A Mirror of Christ ›

Joseph is one of the few Bible characters about whom no major sin or character flaw is recorded. He was not absolutely perfect, but his lifestyle and character were marked by integrity. He kept his life clean and his relationship with God up to date.

The life of Joseph, who was rejected by his family only to save their lives later, has remarkable parallels to the life of Christ.

Match a verse or verses from the life of Jesus to an activity or experience in the life of Joseph. Write the letter of the correct answer on the blank.

LIFE OF JOSEPH	LIFE OF JESUS
1. .... A beloved son	a. Luke 4:8; Hebrews 4:15; 7:26; 1 Peter 2:22
2. .... Gained favor with God and man	b. Luke 4:1–2; Hebrews 2:18

‹ lesson 10 › Jesus—Deliverer for Mankind

3.	.... Obedient to his father	c.	Isaiah 53:3; John 1:10–11
4.	.... Not received by his brothers	d.	Matthew 20:18; 26:2, 14–16; John 13:18
5.	.... Hated and envied	e.	John 1:14; Galatians 4:4
6.	.... Betrayed and sold	f.	John 5:30; 6:38; 17:4
7.	.... Garments taken	g.	Matthew 5:44; Luke 23:34; Romans 5:10
8.	.... Sent away from home	h.	Isaiah 53:7; Matthew 27:12; Mark 15:5
9.	.... Slave/servant	i.	Matthew 27:46
10.	.... Tempted	j.	Luke 2:40, 52
11.	.... Pure, without recorded sin	k.	Mark 12:1–8; 15:10
12.	.... Took undeserved punishment	l.	Matthew 27:35
13.	.... Did not retaliate	m.	Luke 3:22; 9:35
14.	.... Forgotten	n.	Isaiah 53:6, 12; Galatians 3:13; 1 Peter 2:24
15.	.... Exalted by God	o.	Matthew 26:64; Ephesians 1:20–22; Philippians 2:9
16.	.... Enemies bowed before him	p.	Luke 3:23
17.	.... Forgave his enemies	q.	Matthew 20:28; John 13:14; Philippians 2:7
18.	.... Deliverer of the world	r.	Philippians 2:10–11; Revelation 1:7; John 19:37
19.	.... Began to rule at 30 years old	s.	John 1:29; 4:42; 1 John 2:2; 4:14

‹ Building Your Word Knowledge ›

The following exercises explore the meanings of the related words *deliverer*, *redeemer*, and *saviour*.

Below each word, write its English definition.

1. Deliverer

   ....

2. Redeemer

   ....

3. Saviour

   ....

Use *Strong's Concordance* to look up the definitions of the Hebrew and Greek words behind *deliverer*, *redeemer*, and *saviour*; then write the definition next to the word.

4. Deliverer

   a. *yasha`* (H3467) ....

   b. *natsal* (H5337) ....

   c. *palat* (H6403) ....

    d. *lutrotes* (G3084) ....

5. Redeemer
    a. *ga'al* (H1350) ....
    b. *padah* (H6299) ....
    c. *lutroo* (G3084) ....
    d. *agorazo* (G59) ....

6. Saviour
    a. *yasha`* (H3467) ....
    b. *soter* (G4990) ....
    c. *sozo* (G4982) ....

Write your thoughts.

7. Try to write a definition that combines the meanings of the words *deliverer*, *redeemer*, and *saviour*.
....
....

8. How did Joseph fit the definition of a deliverer?
....
....

9. How is Jesus our Deliverer? What does He save us from?
....
....

> "Jesus didn't come to rescue us from our humanity; He entered into humanity to rescue us from our sinfulness." —Joshua Harris[20]

‹ Comparing Scripture with Scripture ›

‹ What Is Sin? ›

1. **Write your definition of sin on the lines below.**
....
....

Sin is disobedience and rebellion against God: "Against thee, thee only, have I sinned, and done this evil in thy sight" (Psalm 51:4). Sin destroys the image of God in oneself and others. Because sin is inconsistent with God's holiness, it separates us from God.

    To be free of sin, we must see it for what it is and refrain from dressing it up with inoffensive labels or excuses.

Look up the references and write your answers.

2. In 1 Samuel 15:23, why is rebellion compared to witchcraft?

   ....

   ....

3. What do our sins withhold from us? (Jeremiah 5:25) ....

4. What have our sins hidden from us? (Isaiah 59:2) ....

5. What have we refused to be? (Jeremiah 3:3) ....

6. What happens if we confess and forsake our sin? (Proverbs 28:13) ....

7. How do you know when an action crosses the line into sin? Where does sin begin? (James 1:14—15; Matthew 5:28)

   ....

   ....

"Take this rule: whatever weakens your reason, impairs the tenderness of your conscience, obscures your sense of God, or takes off the relish of spiritual things; in short, whatever increases the strength and authority of your body over your mind, that thing is sin to you, however innocent it may be in itself."
—Susanna Wesley, to her son John[21]

"Sin does not begin in the physical realm; it begins in the form of desire." —Lisa Bevere[22]

‹ An Impossible Standard? ›

It's easy to justify unrighteousness in our lives by comparing ourselves to others. *Sure, I have some faults, but nobody's perfect. In fact, I know people who are much worse than I am. Yes, I have a bit of a problem, but it's not a sin—at least not a serious one.*

The problem with such thinking is that you are not held accountable for how you compare with others. You are judged by God's standard: the pure and perfect life of Jesus Christ.

But that's impossible!

Yes it is, if you try to do it on your own. However, God offers you His life and power, making it possible to reach His standard while ensuring "that the excellency of the power may be of God, and not of us" (2 Corinthians 4:7).

Look up the references and fill in the blanks.

8. Matthew 5:48 – "Be ye therefore ...."

9. 1 Peter 1:15–16 – "Be ye holy in .... manner of conversation; be ye holy; .... am holy."

10. Philippians 2:15 – ". . . that ye may be .... and ...., the sons of God, without ...."

‹ Causes of Failure ›

If we lose the battle against sin, it is because of one or more of the following reasons:[23]
- We have been holding the wrong standard of holiness.
- We trust the wrong source of power.
- We have the wrong motivations.

Write the correct reference next to the cause of defeat it reveals.

1 Corinthians 6:19–20   Ephesians 5:3   1 John 2:1–2

11. We want to know "how far we can go" and still be holy, when God's standard is perfection.

    ....

12. We trust in our own will power, when only Christ can break the power of sin. ....

13. We think we can conquer lust, make ourselves acceptable to God, and save ourselves. We make ourselves promises and give ourselves punishments in an effort to reform. However, the Law is powerless to save us; it merely shows us God's standard and our depravity and need. Satan wins when our attempts at self-righteousness obscure the righteousness of God.

    We cannot earn righteousness. Instead, we must grasp the life-transforming truth that Christ has already paid our debt of sin. We are saved by the work of Christ, and we are called to live the life of Christ as a response to His work. We have been purchased by God, and we no longer belong to ourselves.

    ....

‹ Power to Overcome ›

Look up the references and fill in the blanks.

14. 1 John 2:1 – "My little children, these things I write unto you, that ye .... not."

15. John 8:11 – "Go, and .... no more."

16. Romans 6:14 – "For sin shall not have .... over you."

17. 1 Corinthians 10:12–13 – "God . . . will with the temptation also make a way to ...."

18. Hebrews 7:25–26 – "He is able also to save them to the .... that come unto God by him."

19. Titus 3:5 – "Not by works of righteousness which .... have done, but according to .... mercy he saved us."

20. 2 Corinthians 5:17 – "Therefore if any man be in Christ, he is a .... creature: old things are passed away; behold, all things are become ...."

21. Colossians 1:27 – "Christ .... you, the hope of glory."

‹ Discussing and Pondering ›

It is not enough to emphasize the *idea* of the cross of Jesus; you must *experience* the cross in your own life. You must die to yourself before you can live for Christ. Romans 7:1–6 teaches that to be "married" to Christ without death to your old life is adultery. You must come to realize that when Jesus died on the cross for your sin, you died with Him. You are dead, and your life is hidden with Christ in God (Colossians 3:3). Jesus not only died, He also rose from the dead and ascended to the Father. Identifying with His death and resurrection allows you to be joined to Christ. Now your life is the result of Christ living in you (Galatians 2:20; 6:14).

God does not want a garden plot that is merely free from weeds; He wants it full of healthy, beautiful plants (John 15:8, 16). Your surrender to Christ begins a process of sanctification as God molds you and begins to work out the life of His Son in you. As long as you follow Him, you are a work in progress.

Are you merely a *professing Christian,* or are you a *practicing* one as well? 1 Peter 2:21 and 1 John 2:6 tell us that our walk must match our profession.

‹ What Is Repentance? ›

Circle the letter of the correct answer.

1. What does it mean to be sorry for my sin?
   a. To feel guilty
   b. To realize the pain my sin brings God and others
   c. To dislike the bad consequences of my sin
   d. To be sorry I got caught

2. What does repentance look like?
   a. A verbal confession of wrongdoing
   b. Telling someone, "I'm sorry if I hurt you."
   c. Changing my behavior and turning away from my sin
   d. A and C

3. Whom does my sin hurt? (2 Samuel 12:9–10, 14)
   a. God
   b. Those I wrong
   c. Me
   d. The people of God
   e. All the above

4. What does it mean to renounce sin?
   a. Ignore that you have it
   b. Give up its right or claim in your life
   c. Declare that it does not exist

"Repentance means to admit it and quit it."
—Joseph Webb

d. Ask God to break its ties in your life

   e. B and D

Some people put all their confidence in the fact that they once prayed a prayer or made a commitment. However, God is concerned about more than your past commitment. He wants you to trust His Deliverer and live for Him now.

‹ Feeling Forgiven ›

To understand God's forgiveness, we need to keep a clear perspective of our Saviour's sacrifice on the cross. It was our sin that drove Him to the cross, and what sin is greater than the sin of crucifying Christ? Yet the price for that ultimate sin has already been paid. God is ready and willing to forgive your sin.

We could never do enough to atone for our sin. It took nothing less than the death of God's perfect Son.[24]

Write your thoughts.

5. Sometimes people say, "I know the Bible says God forgives my sins, but I can't forgive myself for what I did." What do you think they are really saying?

....

....

....

6. Is anyone's sin really too big to be forgiven? ....

Use a concordance to find the reference for this verse.

7. "As far as the east is from the west, so far hath he removed our transgressions from us."

....

‹ Forgiving Others ›

Has someone sinned against you or taken something from you? A proper understanding of what we have been forgiven of makes it possible for us to forgive someone else.

I cannot condemn others for what they have done if I see myself as a fellow sinner in equal need of Christ's atoning death. We are both sinners at the foot of the cross.

I must never use the past as a weapon against those who have hurt me. If God has forgiven, how can I keep clinging to the past? Forgiveness does not mean I no longer feel the pain, but it means offering continual grace and love toward the offender while trusting God to heal my hurts.[25]

> **"And the very God of peace sanctify you wholly; and I pray God your whole spirit and soul and body be preserved blameless unto the coming of our Lord Jesus Christ. Faithful is he that calleth you, who also will do it" (1 Thessalonians 5:23–24).**

Engaging Yourself—Memorization and Application

Jude 1:24–25

As you memorize Jude 1:24–25, use illustrated writing to depict it in the space below (for ideas on illustrating Scripture, review Memorization and Application in Chapter 5).

1. Jude 1:24–25 in illustrated writing:

Complete the following exercises.

2. Have you fully accepted God's deliverance from sin, rejecting your own works and daily trusting Jesus the Deliverer? (John 14:6) ....

3. If you have experienced salvation, write out your thanksgiving for what God has done for you.
....
....
....

4. Share your answer to number 3 above with someone else.

God's Purpose for Joseph

Although Jacob gave Joseph the birthright, the promised Seed came down Judah's line. Jacob loved Joseph's mother, Rachel, and despised Leah, yet God planned that Leah's son Judah would carry the promised Seed. This is an instance of an oft-repeated pattern in history: God favors those whom men despise.

In the plan of God, Joseph did not personally pass on the promised seed, but he did *preserve* the family line of the Deliverer (1 Chronicles 5:1–2; Psalm 78:67–68).

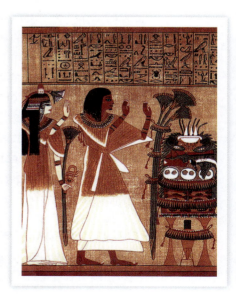

God's choice of the people through whom He would deliver His promises was based on His wisdom and the individual's character, not on birth order. Often, God chose a younger brother over an older one. Isaac, not Ishmael, was the son of promise. Jacob was loved more than Esau. Joseph and Judah were chosen instead of Reuben. Ephraim was placed before Manasseh. David was chosen over his brothers. God's work is not based on birth order or other human measures of status. Rather, He delights in showing His might through the weak and despised (1 Corinthians 1:27–28; 2 Corinthians 12:9).

‹ Quiz 10 ›

Answer *True* or *False*.

1. Joseph was totally perfect and without sin. ....

2. We will fail to keep God's standard if we attempt to do it in our own strength. ....

3. Because Joseph became governor of Egypt and saved his family, he was chosen as the one through whom the Messiah would one day come. ....

Write the answer in the blank.

4. What expression is sometimes used to describe the eternal theme of salvation woven throughout the Bible?
   ....

5. What two titles are synonyms of *deliverer*? ....

6. List five ways Joseph and Jesus Christ were similar.
   a. ....
   b. ....
   c. ....
   d. ....
   e. ....

7. What does the following sentence mean? "It is not enough to emphasize the *idea* of the cross of Jesus; you must *experience* the cross in your own life."
   ....
   ....
   ....

8. By whose standard will we be held to account? ....

Fill in the blanks.

9. "Repentance means to admit it and ...."

10. Write Jude 1:24–25 from memory.
   ....
   ....
   ....
   ....

‹ part two ›

LESSON BACKGROUND MATERIAL

LESSON 1
Family Influences

‹ Analyzing God's Word ›

Joseph's Family

Joseph's family were nomadic shepherds living as strangers in a land that had been promised to them by God, but which they did not yet own. They moved from place to place, living in tents and seeking food and water for their animals.

Joseph's father had several wives. The relational tensions in this blended family produced many opportunities for turmoil and heartache. Jealousy and favoritism tore Joseph's family apart.

Joseph's father, Jacob, had begun his adult life with a "bargain" that if God would prosper him and bring him home safely after he fled his brother's anger, he would make the LORD his God. He consistently referred to the LORD as the "God of my fathers," not as his own God.

Genesis 29–30

Jacob was known as a deceiver willing to trample others to come out on top. He deceived his own father, stealing the blessing from his brother Esau and angering him so deeply that Jacob had to flee for his life. But in his conniving, Jacob did not always come out on top. His uncle Laban tricked him into marrying Leah, the sister of Rachel, the girl he loved. In the end, he married Rachel as well, but in return he had to serve his uncle another seven years.

Polygamy was never God's will or design. Although in this Old Testament period God allowed this practice because of people's ignorance, we can see that this sinful relationship brought much pain into Jacob's home. When Jesus was questioned about marriage, He pointed back to Creation to show that God's intention has not changed. His purpose for marriage is one man and one woman for life.

Joseph and his brothers were caught in a family war,

Crosa of Nuernberg

as two jealous sisters vied for the attention and love of their husband. Joseph's mother, Rachel, could not have children for many years, and in their society, barrenness was considered a great disgrace. Leah bore Jacob sons, placing her at a social advantage over her sister, but never winning her the love she wanted.

In competition, each of the two sisters gave her servant girl to Jacob as an additional partner, hoping the surrogate mother would bear children that her mistress could claim as her own. However, although Rachel's servant bore children, this did not bring Rachel satisfaction. The children inherited their mothers' rivalry, and when Rachel finally had a son, Joseph, Jacob favored him above all his ten brothers, since his mother was the beloved wife.

Genesis 31

When Joseph was six years old, the family decided to return from Haran to the land of Canaan. Because of the animosity between Jacob and his uncle Laban, they secretly fled from Laban's home. Rachel, assuming that their manner of leaving would cost her the inheritance, stole her father's household idols, which seemed to be connected with the title deeds of inheritance.[26] Aside from God's intervention, Laban surely would have attacked Jacob's family in retaliation when he learned of their departure.

Genesis 32–33

As Jacob's family approached their home in Canaan, Jacob's brother Esau came to meet them with four hundred armed men. Fearing that Esau meant revenge, Jacob split up the company, hoping to give some a chance to escape if they were attacked. Then he prepared a large gift as a gesture of peace to his brother. However, the most important thing Jacob did during this frightening time was to seek the blessing of God. Through this experience, Jacob learned to trust God instead of his own strength and conniving. This appears to be the beginning of Jacob's personal relationship with God. Here God changed his name from Jacob (grasper, deceiver) to Israel (prince with God). The family experienced God's protection when Esau graciously met them in peace.

A Man God Trusted

Psalm 53:2 says, "God looked down from heaven upon the children of men, to see if there were any that did understand, that did seek God." In Genesis we see that in Joseph, God found a man to fill His purposes. God was pleased with Joseph. He had certain plans that only a strong man could handle (Proverbs 24:10; Isaiah 40:30–31; Lamentations 3:24–27). God knew Joseph could be trusted to bear tremendous trials without crumbling, so God used him to preserve life and save the lineage of the Deliverer of mankind from extinction.

Violent Kin

Genesis 33:17–35:15

After leaving Haran, where Joseph was born, the family settled for a time at Succoth, near Shechem. Jacob bought a small field from Shechem's father, thus laying claim to the promise of God that his seed would possess the land (Genesis 12:5–8). At Succoth, Jacob built an altar and called it *Elelohe-Israel* (God the God of Israel).

Jacob's daughter (Joseph's half-sister) Dinah made the grave mistake of going out alone to visit the girls of the land. While she was away from home, Prince Shechem, struck by her beauty, took her and defiled her. Afterward, he remained so taken with Dinah that he approached Jacob and the brothers with a request for marriage.

The angry brothers deceived Shechem and his people by promising peace and intermarriage on the condition that the men of Shechem become circumcised as they were. All the men of the city agreed and came under the knife, and while they were laid up, Simeon and Levi killed them and plundered the city to avenge the defilement of their sister.

Jacob was distraught; he feared the massacre would invite revenge from the other inhabitants of the land. But God called the family of Jacob to return to Bethel, "The House of God," and renew their vows. In preparation for this journey, the whole family discarded their idols. The Lord caused fear to fall on the nations around them, and they did them no harm. At Bethel, Jacob's family built an altar, and God confirmed the Abrahamic Covenant with Israel.

Genesis 35:16–29

After leaving Bethel, Rachel, the beloved wife, died while giving birth to her second son, Benjamin. Now there were a total of twelve sons.

A great contrast existed between Joseph and his brothers—a contrast greater than the one created by their father's favoritism toward Joseph. In this part of the story, we begin to notice the differences in their character. God blessed Joseph not because he was his father's favorite son, but because he had a different character from his brothers. He lived a life God could bless.

Reuben, the eldest brother, went in and lay with his father's concubine, Bilhah. This defilement brought a reproach (shame) on him. His father could no longer trust him, and he lost the blessing of the firstborn (I Chronicles 5:1–2). Jacob always seemed to hold Simeon and Levi's cruelty to the men of Shechem against them. Judah also had great moral failings in his family.

Sibling Rivalry

Genesis 37

At the age of seventeen, Joseph was sent to herd sheep with the sons of Bilhah and Zilpah. The phrase "feeding the flocks" carries the idea that he was the main shepherd over the flock, implying that Joseph was placed in a position of leadership over his older brothers.[27] While Joseph was with them, his brothers were involved in some kind of sin, although the Bible does not record what it was. Joseph apparently refused to join in his brothers' wrongdoing, and he reported it to their father. While this may have been the right thing to do, it seems certain that the brothers resented it.

Jacob seemed bent on passing the birthright to Joseph, his beloved son. He gave him the honorary "coat of many colors," showing his intention to treat Joseph as his firstborn. Everyone could see that Jacob loved Joseph best, and his brothers were consumed with hate and envy. Jacob should have known from his own boyhood experience that favoritism brings heartache.

> **God knew what turmoil lay in store for Joseph, and He gave him a special promise and hope to cling to.**

In the midst of spite and hate, Joseph had two vivid dreams that foretold a time when he would rule over his brothers. These were no common dreams; they were given by God to reveal that He had a plan for Joseph's life. Nothing could thwart the fulfilment of this dream—not mockery, hatred, slavery, enticements, or prison. Joseph would be able to look back and see that his life was not a series of coincidences, but the work of a loving, providential God.

Why did Joseph share his dreams with his jealous brothers? Perhaps he was ignorant or naive. Perhaps it was the will of God to bring about His purposes and to influence the brothers. Whatever Joseph's reasons for telling his dreams, it made his brothers hate him even

Trish Steel

more, but his father remembered these messages.

Much of the hatred Joseph experienced resulted from the way his pure life accentuated the faults of his brothers. They were angered by the implication that he would one day rule over them, yet they must have known there was nothing to disqualify him, for he lived a better life than they did.

Joseph willingly obeyed when his father trusted him with the dangerous responsibility of going to see how his brothers were doing. The brothers were feeding the flocks sixty miles to the north, near Shechem, where they had once slaughtered the men of the city. Jacob may have been concerned that the people of the land would harm his sons, or perhaps he did not trust them to stay out of trouble.

The danger to Joseph arose not from the people around Shechem or from wild animals, but from his own brothers' hatred. Even as he approached them, they began plotting how to get rid of him. Several of them felt uneasy about committing outright murder, so they agreed to pitch Joseph into a dry cistern to die a slow death. Reuben secretly planned to return and free Joseph later, but before he could do so, a caravan of Midianite traders passed, and the other brothers decided to get some money out of the deal by selling Joseph as a slave. They all conspired to take Joseph's special coat, dip it in the blood of a goat, and present it to their father to convince him that a wild animal had devoured Joseph. They would live this lie for twenty years.

Security in God

Joseph could have used all these experiences as an excuse to reject God, to give in to temptation, or to indulge in self-pity. Yet he was true to God, even in the midst of painful family conflict, never viewing hardships as an excuse for failure. Joseph did not allow the example of his family to mold his character. He did not blame his problems on his upbringing or influences.

The things that happened to Joseph did not determine his life's direction. He was not a victim of his past. Instead, he chose a higher calling. His integrity was displayed by his refusal to follow the examples of deception, thievery, disrespect, favoritism, jealousy, hate, greed, moral impurity, pride, and revenge practiced by others in his family. He chose, with God's help, not to follow these negative patterns.

Today, God is looking for faithful men and women. Those who remain steadfast through hard trials can be trusted to take on great responsibility. What will His verdict be regarding you?

"And I sought for a man among them, that should make up the hedge, and stand in the gap before me for the land, that I should not destroy it" (Ezekiel 22:30).

‹ Building Your Word Knowledge ›

The Blessing of Children

In Bible times, children were highly valued. Childlessness was considered a disgrace and a curse. Although many people today see children as an obstacle to success, a godly perspective allows us to see children for the great blessing they are.

Children can fill a house with life and potential. They become your comfort and strength in old age. They carry on your legacy after you are gone. People are the only investments that will last. Possessions cannot be taken with you, but children are forever. Children trained in obedience are a parent's pride and glory.

"Lo, children are an heritage of the Lord: and the fruit of the womb is his reward" (Psalm 127:3). Our society despises what God honors and honors what God despises!

Children are also a defense, like long-range weapons that extend your reach. "As arrows are in the hand of a mighty man; so are children of the youth. Happy is the man that hath his quiver full of them: they shall not be ashamed, but they shall speak with the enemies in the gate" (Psalm 127:4–5).

Joseph Hall recalls, "I remember a great man coming into my house at Waltham, and seeing all my children standing in the order of their age and stature, said, 'These are they that make rich men poor.'

"But he straight received this answer, 'Nay, my lord, these are they that make a poor man rich; for there is not one of these whom we would part with for all your wealth.' " —Charles Spurgeon[a]

‹ Comparing Scripture with Scripture ›

If you have a study Bible, you may have cross-references listed after each verse or in the margin of the text. These point to other verses on related topics. The *Treasury of Scripture Knowledge* is an extensive cross-reference resource you may want to use. You may also look up the words *name* or *character* in a topical Bible, such as *Nave's Topical Bible,* or a similar study aid.

---

[a] From *The Treasury of David*

‹ Discussing and Pondering ›

Consider the following topics.

Was polygamy okay in Old Testament times? What is God's will for marriage and family? Read and consider Acts 17:30 and Mark 10:2–12.

Is it ever okay to tattle or tell on someone who does wrong? Consider Psalm 50:18; 2 John 1:10–11; 1 Timothy 5:22; and Romans 1:32. We are cautioned against aiding, encouraging, or blessing others in their sin. If you know someone's sin and cover for him, you become guilty as well. By doing nothing, you are an accomplice to his deed.

More questions to think about:

- Why do you think God gave Joseph these two dreams that provoked such jealousy?
- Joseph was honored by an extravagant coat. Have you ever been tempted to flaunt your gifts and blessings? Do these things make you better than those around you?
- Think about Joseph's character and the characters of his brothers. How was Joseph different from his brothers? Why?
- Proverbs 20:11 tells us that even a child is known by his "doings"—his character. How does one build a good reputation? How quickly can it be destroyed?
- How does jealousy take root in our hearts? What are its results?

Additional activity:

Use a baby name book or web site to look up your own name. Is there a character quality or life verse that goes with your name? Look for a passage in the Bible that captures the character quality given in the meaning. You may need to be creative in connecting meanings to positive traits. Ask God for vision.

‹ Engaging Yourself— Memorization and Application ›

Suggested Reading

The Genesis Record, by Henry Morris (devotional commentary on the book of Genesis)

LESSON 2
Trials and Disappointments

‹ Analyzing God's Word ›
Genesis 37, 39–40

The Venom of Hatred and Jealousy

Joseph was favored by his father in ways that angered his brothers. Although this was beyond Joseph's control, he had a superior character, and his pure life only accentuated the shortcomings of his brothers. When he shared the dreams God had given him—that he would someday be a ruler—his brothers became even angrier. They made up their minds that this would never happen.

Joseph's brothers were angry at the thought of him ruling, not because he was unqualified, but because he was qualified and they were not. They seemed to know he was capable of ruling over them, and they were determined not to allow it. Joseph's brothers envied him and could not even speak peaceably to him.

Joseph was not only favored by his father, but he was also obedient. Knowing that his brothers despised him, it is amazing that he willingly went alone, at his father's request, to check on their safety. He persisted in the task until he finally located his brothers at Dothan. However, they were not pleased to see him.

The Fruit of Bitterness and Jealousy

The brothers' first impulse was to kill Joseph outright. Reuben, however, felt some responsibility as the eldest brother and persuaded the others to throw Joseph into a dry cistern so they would not be guilty of shedding his blood. They viciously tore his distinctive, colorful coat from him, threw him into the pit, and then callously sat down to eat.

Although Reuben planned to release Joseph, he never

Michael Ely

had the opportunity. While he was out of camp, some Midianite traders came by. Consumed by their desire to prevent Joseph's dreams from coming true, his brothers conceived the idea of selling him to the traders.

Genesis 42:21 tells us the brothers saw the anguish of Joseph's soul, but they ignored him. When he wept and pled with them, they would not listen. Joseph watched as his brothers sold him like an animal for twenty silver coins. After the traders led Joseph away, his brothers tore and stained his coat with goat blood to convince their father that he had been devoured by a wild animal.

What would become of his dreams now?

Joseph, stripped of all his rights, was on his way to Egypt to be sold as a slave. He must have battled hopelessness as he realized that his father would not know where he was, or even that he was alive. He would never be rescued.

To a young person, it can seem unfair to lose the security of a parent's protection. Joseph could have felt rejected by his father. He might have wondered why his father had sent him to his brothers; after all, his father knew they hated him.

Joseph could have easily felt forgotten and rejected by God.

Thrust into a new culture with strange customs, language, and religion, Joseph could have wondered where God was. Did God even know he was suffering? Did He care? Was He in control? Was He even real? Joseph's dreams must have seemed like a mockery now. Why should he trust God anymore?

Choosing to Serve

People often blame God when they face trials. Did Joseph fall into self-pity or spiral into depression? Did he become morose, sullen, and bitter? Did he reject God?

Martyn Gorman

No! He placed his hope in God. He trusted that God was in control of his life and that whatever God chose to do was good.

In his new life, Joseph made the most of every situation. He always sought to bless those around him. He did not seek revenge or lash out at others in his pain.

Even as a common slave, Joseph used his talents to bless his new master. Because of Joseph's faithfulness, he was entrusted with great responsibility, and God used him to bless the household of an Egyptian ruler.

When Joseph responded righteously and glorified God in this difficult situation, did things get better? No, there was more trouble ahead.

Because of another person's lust, Joseph was tempted, framed, and accused of assaulting his master's wife. He found himself a prisoner in chains—thrown into a dungeon on false charges. Egypt's treatment of political prisoners was severe (Psalm 105:18), so Joseph was faced with pain, confining walls, and the unfairness of his position.

However, Joseph again chose to trust God and serve others. The jailer must have recognized his character, if not his innocence, for he gave Joseph control over many of the prison's affairs. Joseph reached out to others who were suffering and offered them hope. He served them. It seems that Potiphar (the captain of the guard) still had some oversight in Joseph's life, for he placed two political prisoners under his charge.[b] Joseph served these men faithfully, and his interpretation of their dreams earned him a debt of gratitude from Pharaoh's butler. However, the butler totally forgot Joseph for two years after being released.

Throughout this time, God was Joseph's source of stability, and Joseph continued walking in integrity and faithfulness. God dwells only with those whose hearts are prepared, and the best accolade the Scripture gives about Joseph is this: ". . . but God was with him" (Acts 7:9).

‹ Building Your Word Knowledge ›

Here are some very basic things we assume are ours, but which can be taken from us at any time: strength, ability, intelligence, good looks, family, health, and even the breath of life. These are all gifts from God (Psalm 104:27–29).

---

[b] As Pharaoh's executioner, Potiphar would have had authority over the prison where Joseph was in custody, although Joseph was not directly accountable to him. Word of Joseph's behavior in prison would likely have reached Potiphar throughout the time Joseph was there.

If we think we are exercising our rights, we need to pay close attention to our motives. Are we really concerned about what is right, or are we just seeking our own convenience or comfort?

To experience God's blessing, we must yield up our "rights" to His wisdom. Who are we to argue with our Creator or accuse Him of unfairness? He deserves our service not because we approve of what He does, but because He is a righteous God (Job 2:10; 1:22). He has the right to mold and use us as He sees fit.

‹ Discussing and Pondering ›

There are two ways you may feel pain or rejection from others: someone may say or do specific things that hurt you, or someone may neglect or fail you.

God does not take pleasure in seeing us suffer. He hurts with us, but He will not take away our pain, because the suffering is worth the joy of learning to depend on Him and becoming like Christ.

The Value of Trials[28]

- They increase your awareness of others' needs.
- They teach you to become more loving and helpful to others.
- They lead you into new and lasting friendships.
- They teach you humility.
- They teach you patience.
- They deepen your maturity and build endurance.
- They purify your motives and smooth off the rough edges of your character.
- They force you to learn new skills.
- They are platforms for leadership.
- They increase your understanding of and love for God.
- They teach you wisdom. You can learn even from failures—both yours and others'.
- They encourage you to leave a greater legacy than you received.

Illustration:

Joseph found himself in a pit. Use a play on words by bringing a peach or cherry pit to your class. Discuss the worth of a pit. What does the pit represent to you? Is it symbolic of missed opportunities, discarded pleasure, death, or shattered dreams? Or does it remind you that God can bring life from something that seems dead? Does it promise hope of new life and future fruit? (John 11:25–26; 12:24)

Additional activity:

Study the words of the song, "More Love to Thee" by Elizabeth Prentiss.

‹ Engaging Yourself— Memorization and Application ›

Suggested Reading

Walking Through Shadows, by Ken Ham and Carl Wieland (on the "whys" of suffering)

LESSON 3

Respect, Honor, and Obedience

‹ Analyzing God's Word ›

Genesis 37, 39–41

As a Son

God highly values obedience to parents. Of the Ten Commandments, the command to honor parents is the only one linked with a blessing or a curse.

Joseph's noble life brought great pleasure to his father. Jacob trusted Joseph with great responsibilities, not only because he was the son of his beloved Rachel, but also because of his clean, obedient, and faithful life. Joseph's character was more important to Jacob than his place in the birth order.

The obedience of Joseph is much like that of Christ. Matthew 3:17 and John 5:30 show how Jesus' obedient life brought pleasure to His Father, as Joseph's did to Jacob.

Jacob kept giving greater and greater responsibilities to Joseph. At seventeen years old, he was placed in charge of a portion of the flocks, and possibly given authority over some of his older brothers. Later, when the brothers were feeding the flocks near Shechem, the city where they had committed the massacre, Jacob sent Joseph to check on them. As mentioned in chapter two, Joseph obeyed although he knew his brothers hated him, and he went further than many young men would by persisting until he found them.

As a Slave

As a slave, Joseph found freedom in willingly serving those in authority over him.[29] He was free to bless Potiphar and increase his master's possessions. Although he did not choose to be a slave, he chose to serve well in that capacity. Joseph had learned to cheerfully obey instructions even when it did not seem in his best interests to do so. Now he continued to trust the safety and blessing of God by obeying his authorities, even in situations that seemed hard or unfair. Choosing to remain under the umbrella of God's authority structure brings us protection from evil, though it does not guarantee freedom from hardships. God will honor willing submission, even if it brings us temporary suffering.

It was because of Joseph's hard work and willing heart that God blessed Potiphar's household. Joseph was free from bitterness and did not malign his master or stir up rebellion against him. Joseph focused not on his own feelings, but on the good of others. He gladly helped build Potiphar's reputation and wealth.

When we please God, others will take notice. People want to be near someone God is blessing. Joseph caught the attention of the people around him, just as Jesus in His youth increased in wisdom, stature, and favor with God and man (Luke 2:52).

No matter whom he was serving, Joseph respected his authorities. When one of his superiors asked Joseph to sin, he remained obedient to the higher authority

of Potiphar, and ultimately to the highest authority—God. Even though God's law trumps all others, Joseph appealed to God's law respectfully, without rudeness or arrogance, when he refused to commit adultery with Potiphar's wife.

As a Prisoner

Even in prison, Joseph's servant heart was evident, standing in contrast to all the bitterness, self-pity, and misery there. In the midst of his pain, he sought to bless and serve others. Despite his circumstances, his positive, cheerful outlook soon earned him a promotion, and he was put in charge of everything done in the prison.

As a Ruler

Even when Joseph appealed for release, he did not accuse or malign his authorities (Genesis 40:15). Further, while Joseph wanted to be free, he was not seeking power, and when he received it, he held it lightly, respecting those under his authority as well as those over him.

True respect is shown by how you treat those below you in rank. Joseph treated the people of Egypt with kindness and fairness. When they came to buy grain, he honored their personhood and preserved their dignity by charging fair prices and offering ways to earn the food they needed. He did not prey on their desperation. Joseph's management made it possible for the people to support themselves once the famine was over, rather than passively depending on handouts.

Even as a ruler, Joseph remained accountable to Pharaoh. Pharaoh did not feel threatened by Joseph's power and popularity, because Joseph worked for Pharaoh's success, not his own (Genesis 47:26). Years later, when Joseph wanted to travel to Canaan for the burial of his father, he first secured Pharaoh's blessing.

Joseph never grew too big to bow. Before the death of his father, Joseph brought his two sons to visit their grandfather and be blessed by him. In Genesis 48:12 we see the great ruler, Zaphnath-paaneah, bowing with his face to the earth before his father. Joseph respected his father throughout his life, and even at the time of his father's death, he honored him and carried out his wishes.

God honors those who honor their parents as Joseph did. In Jeremiah 35:1–19 we read of a family known as the Rechabites, who were blessed by God and held up as an example to Israel for honoring the command of their father long after he was gone.

‹ Discussing and Pondering ›

Thoughts on "Tough Questions" exercise:

What should you do when someone in authority tells you to do something morally wrong? Does being obedient mean you must do whatever you're told without question, regardless of your conscience?

Jesus' disciples faced this in Acts 5:28–29.

First, make sure the demand is truly wrong and that you are not just looking for an excuse to avoid doing something you don't want to do. Second, always appeal to and obey the highest authority. God is over every human authority. Third, maintain a respectful attitude even if you must disobey an authority in order to obey God.

Joseph tried to be obedient and respectful, but when

he had to choose, he obeyed God rather than man. Romans 12:18 admonishes us, "As much as lieth in you, live peaceably with all men." As much as you can, be obedient to those in authority.

Do not confuse a simple lack of wisdom with moral wrong. Not every foolish thing is sinful. It may be tempting to overstep your own boundaries to save a leader from a "dumb choice," especially if you think the consequences might hurt you. But it pleases God more if you offer a suggestion and then are willing to suffer if the leader makes the wrong choice. Don't take others' authority away. Your call is to honor and obey them as far as you can within God's commands, not to come out on top.

Does submitting to someone make you less important than that person?

No, it does not. 1 Corinthians 11:3 says God is the head of Christ. That does not make Christ any less God. Likewise, the head of woman is man. This headship order refers to responsibilities and roles, not importance or value.

God has placed an order of headship or authority within our homes and society. Being a leader does not mean making decisions all alone, but leadership does mean being responsible for final decisions and their consequences. All leaders will one day stand before God to give account for how they led (Hebrews 13:17).

Are you called to respect people who are wrong? What if they have hurt you or failed to protect you? Do you still need to honor them?

There are several ways you may feel hurt by others, leading you to consider them undeserving of honor. Someone may have done an act against you, such as physical or verbal abuse, or they may have hurt you through neglect or rejection—failing you when you needed them.

Honoring someone does not mean approving everything they do or excusing their sin. Rather, honor is a value we place on a person independent of their performance. Honor means recognizing that the other is a fellow person made by God even though he is imperfect.[30] Our authorities deserve our honor because God has placed them in a role of responsibility. The way of God is to treat others as we *want* to be treated—not as we *have* been treated (Luke 6:31–36).

Is honor something others must earn before you give it?

The honor, respect, and obedience God calls for is not dependent on the performance of others. God does not say "Honor your parents—unless they are unfair or abusive." Although it is hard to honor those you do not respect, it is a command, not an optional recommendation.

Just as sin begins with the attitudes of the heart, so does honor. It is a choice you make. Once you have committed to show someone honor, you will find ways to do it.

"Like genuine love, honor is a gift we give to someone. It involves the decision we make *before* we put love into action that a person is of high value. In fact, love for someone often begins to flow once we have made the decision to honor him."[31]

Honoring someone who does not seem to deserve it is much easier when we recognize that trials have value—that God has a good plan. Joseph was sold as a slave, framed for adultery, thrown into jail without a trial, forgotten by the one who could have worked for his release; yet he said, "You meant it for evil, but God meant it for good."

‹ Engaging Yourself— Memorization and Application ›

"Servants, be subject to your masters with all fear; not only to the good and gentle, but also to the froward" (1 Peter 2:18).

You Can Show Honor to Others by . . .
- valuing them highly and lifting them up.
- speaking affirming words.
- blessing and the laying on of hands, with words of affirmation.

- being careful not to treat their achievements and thoughts as stupid or unimportant.
- doing gracious deeds.
- making it a priority to take time for them.
- carrying out their wishes.
- being unselfish.
- acting wisely—Proverbs tells us wise children are an honor to parents, while foolish ones bring them shame.
- protecting the reputation of those in authority over us.
- focusing on the success of others rather than our own.

Most Parents Would Feel Honored If You Would . . . [32]

- call, write, or send a card sometime besides Mother's or Father's Day.
- hug them when you plan to leave or when you return (even if they aren't the hugging type).
- do what needs to be done without being told to do it.
- help others less fortunate than you.
- ask their advice.
- be truthful with them (in a kind way), even if you disagree.
- pray for them.
- do your best in your personal undertakings; your actions reflect on them.
- seek God with all your heart.
- discuss "taboo" subjects with them, such as drinking, sex, and drugs.
- defend them when others accuse them behind their backs.
- assure them of your love.
- care for them as they grow older.
- be grateful and say "Thank you."

Common courtesies that show honor:

- Look at someone when you are speaking to them or they are speaking to you.
- Use respectful body language when talking with others. (Don't slouch in your seat, roll your eyes, exhale loudly, or cross your arms.) Practice respectful body language even if the other person cannot see you.
- Show an interest in what others are saying. Don't cut them off to answer the phone, send a text, or check email.
- Do not interrupt. Wait for your turn to speak.
- Listen attentively to others and restate their words to ensure that you understand.
- Hold the door open or step out of someone's path.
- Offer assistance.
- Take extra measures to value and serve the elderly.[c] Stand before the aged person.
- Give up your seat to a woman, a handicapped person, or someone older than you.
- Where appropriate, use an honorary title (Mr., Mrs., Sir, Ma'am).
- Look out for others before yourself.

Suggested Reading

The Gift of Honor, by Gary Smalley and John Trent
Practicing Affirmation, by Sam Crabtree

---

[c] Leviticus 19:32 says, "Thou shalt rise up before the hoary (gray) head, and honour the face of the old man." In modern U.S. society, we do not often see actions of courtesy when an older person comes into the room. Can we recapture this practice?

LESSON 4

Moral Purity

‹ Analyzing God's Word ›

Genesis 39

Why should Joseph remain true to the ideals he had been taught? He was alone, far from home, and no one around him cared whether he was upright or not.

Joseph's brothers were a bunch of hypocrites who sinned behind their father's back and thought nothing of betraying Joseph. His father had put him at risk by sending him alone to his brothers when they were known to hate him. Why should he be faithful to his family or their God?

No one in Joseph's family had been a good example of integrity and godliness. His father had used deception when it was convenient, and even his grandfather Isaac and great-grandfather Abraham had lied to save their own skins. The family had been plagued by repeated immorality. How could Joseph be expected to be godly and pure?

Besides all this, Joseph was now a slave of Potiphar,[33] an officer of Pharaoh. Obedience to his master was critical. He could have reasoned that he was not accountable for what he did, since he was just following orders.

Living for the Audience of One [d]

The most important thing Joseph took with him to Egypt was the awareness that God was with him, watching him and guiding him. He knew that no matter where he was, God saw him. This knowledge did not frighten him; he wanted to please God.

With pleasing God as his goal, Joseph lived an exem-

plary life. He was faithful and honest in everything he did. God blessed Joseph; when Potiphar saw how he prospered in everything he did, he made Joseph overseer of his entire household. Potiphar trusted Joseph so completely, he did not even check up on his work.

The tables had turned for the Hebrew slave. Joseph had power and good looks. He was at his physical peak, probably in his early twenties. Attracted to him, Potiphar's beautiful wife approached him and offered herself to him for pleasure.

---

[d] The term *Audience of One* is gleaned from Randy Alcorn's book, *Safely Home*.

Living with No Regrets

Sensual pleasure is a strong attraction for any young man, but for Joseph, the danger of crossing this woman's will may have been an even stronger inducement to sin. His master's wife had much power over Joseph's future. What would she do if he refused her offer?

Beyond the temptation to outright sin, Joseph may have been tempted to feel he was strong enough to entertain the idea.

Many people feel as though fleeing from a temptation is some kind of weakness. They tell themselves, *I can handle this.* Are you tempted to entertain sin—to dialogue with it? Flirting with sin, getting as close as we can, carries a certain euphoria. Often people think they can play around with sin but still say no. How did Joseph handle the temptation of his master's wife?

He flat-out refused. Joseph recognized that he had been given great responsibility. He controlled everything Potiphar owned except his wife, and Joseph had no right to her. Above all, it would be great wickedness

Linda Spashett

and a sin against God. However, refusing the temptation once did not put the matter to rest. His master's wife did not give up. She tried to wear him down by daily invitations. Still, "He hearkened not unto her, to lie by her, or to be with her" (Genesis 39:10).

A typical Egyptian house included a connected granary, workshops, and kitchens. These portions of the house usually lay behind the private halls. Joseph's duties regularly took him through the house's living quarters, so he could not avoid the temptation.

Potiphar's wife was watching for her opportunity. One day while all the other men were out (possibly by her direction), she caught Joseph alone in the house. The trap was sprung! She grabbed his clothing, intending to leave him no choice but to commit immorality with her.

This time Joseph did not try to reason with his master's wife. After a struggle, he tore loose from his clothing (a simple wrap-around garment), leaving it in her hands, and fled the house.

Thwarted desire often turns to hatred. Jealousy demands, "If I can't have what I want, no one else will have it either." Furious, Potiphar's wife accused Joseph of the very thing she had tried to do, claiming that Joseph had tried to rape her. She had his clothing with her as proof that Joseph had broken his trust. She told this lie to the whole household, including Potiphar when he returned. Jealousy and lies are hateful!

Potiphar's wrath boiled over, and he threw Joseph into prison. So much for Joseph's efforts to do right!

From a human perspective, we focus on the immediate trouble Joseph experienced; he was falsely accused, his reputation was destroyed, he lost his job, and he was thrown into prison. Taking God's perspective, however, we can see that Joseph's godly choices did have some immediate rewards—he remained pure, and God was pleased with him!

In our society, purity is valued so little that it's hard for us to see it as its own wonderful reward for faithfulness, but it is a real treasure. Even though the immediate rewards of righteousness and purity are not always obvious, they are real, and we are called to be faithful.

‹ Building Your Word Knowledge ›

Strong's Exhaustive Concordance is available as a large printed book and in various digital forms; for example, I enjoy using the Power Bible software from Online Publishing, which includes *Strong's* and many other dictionaries, translations, and commentaries.

It may be helpful for a teacher to assist first-time users

of *Strong's Concordance*.

Some synonyms for *integrity* are *honesty, truth, honor, reliability,* and *uprightness*.

‹ Comparing Scripture with Scripture ›

"The law of the wise is a fountain of life, to depart from the snares of death. Good understanding giveth favour: but the way of transgressors is hard" (Proverbs 13:14–15).

Illustration:
Slowly push a book toward the edge of the table while saying, "God, don't let it fall; don't let it fall." When the book hits the floor, ask why God allowed it to fall. Why didn't He stop it? Even though God is able to keep us from sinning, He will not remove our free will if we insist on playing with sin. God provides the strength to say no when we obey the warnings He gives us.[34]

‹ Engaging Yourself— Memorization and Application ›

"Blessed are the pure in heart: for they shall see God" (Matthew 5:8).

Guarding with Diligence

Ways Men and Women Can Guard Their Hearts

- Do not trust yourself alone with temptation.
- Watch what you fill your eyes and mind with. Do not let yourself become snared by pornography.
- Learn to *avert your eyes* from temptation. (Do not listen to the lie that looking at immoral pictures is not sin, since they are not real people. If it stimulates lust and you dwell on it, it is sin.)
- Realize that fantasizing is also a form of pornography. Fantasy obsesses your mind with what you do not have. All sin begins when we fail to control the desires of the heart. (See 1 Peter 1:13.)
- Starve temptation. Whenever possible, refuse to go places where you know you will be tempted.
- Do not give your heart to every new person who expresses an interest in you. If you allow yourself to become a cheap thrill because you are desperate for love, you will likely settle for lust rather than love. An easy catch is not a highly-honored treasure.
- Realize that close friendships formed via email, texting, Facebook, etc., with people you don't know in real life, can seem very special, yet be shallow and fake in reality.
- Using your body to catch someone may very well catch you the *wrong* person. Immodest clothes or actions send the message: "Look at me. I'm available!" If you train someone to look at you mainly for sensual pleasure, what will keep their interest from roving to other people's bodies after marriage?
- Realize that sex is more than just the physical act—it is intended by God to be a very deep and bonding experience, emotionally and spiritually.
- Realize that saving yourself for your future spouse is a special gift.
- Be faithful to your spouse. Do him or her good *all* the days of your life—even while single. Ask yourself, "Am I loving and protecting the one I may someday marry?" (Proverbs 31:11–12)
- Realize that you cannot conquer temptation in your own power. Cry out to God!
- Identify your points of weakness and fortify yourself.
- Be accountable to others. Pray for others who are tempted in similar areas.
- Memorize 2 Corinthians 10:5 and Philippians 4:8. Wash your mind through exposure to Scripture. Choose passages that will help you combat specific temptations you face.
- Specifically commit your conscious and subconscious thoughts to God.

- Establish wholesome friendships and activities.
- Commit to keep yourself for God and your mate. Men should be leaders in the practice of purity.
- Take your mind off yourself; learn to serve others!

Ways Couples Can Guard Their Relationship

- Ask God to make your spouse the most desirable person in the world to you.
- Communicate by seeking to understand and care about each other's experiences and perspectives. Listen to each other's hearts.
- Be fiercely loyal to and speak highly of your spouse.
- Seek to serve, rather than be served.
- Be content with the person God has given you (Proverbs 5:15-20; Hebrews 13:4).
- Protect against "casual" close friendships with others of the opposite gender. When you say "I do" to one, you are saying "No" to everyone else.
- Guard yourself against pornography, whether in pictures, movies, or novels. A husband cannot compete with the perfectly sensitive and romantic men in romance novels. A wife's body can never compete with the airbrushed bodies in photos. The fake people and relationships depicted by porn set an impossible standard that can ruin your enjoyment of the real thing.
- Do not be soft on your sin. King Solomon observed that it was the "little foxes" that spoiled the vines (Song of Solomon 2:15). Deal with sin immediately, consistently, and ruthlessly.

"We know that whosoever is born of God sinneth not; but he that is begotten of God keepeth himself, and that wicked one toucheth him not" (1 John 5:18).

Suggested Reading

The Purity Principle, by Randy Alcorn
Not Even a Hint/Sex Is Not the Problem (Lust Is), by Joshua Harris
I Kissed Dating Goodbye, by Joshua Harris
Boy Meets Girl, by Joshua Harris
Passion and Purity, by Elizabeth Elliot
Quest for Love, by Elizabeth Elliot

LESSON 5

Samson: A Life of Dishonor

‹ Analyzing God's Word ›

Judges 13–16

At first glance it seems that the lives of Joseph and Samson were about as opposite as they could be, but many of the temptations they faced were similar; it was their response to these temptations that was different. To Joseph, purity and integrity were values to be prized; to Samson, they were inconveniences to be endured.

The call on Samson came even before he was born. God had a specific task for Samson's life and specific requirements for his conduct. God wanted him to live a life dedicated to purity and separated from sin for His purposes.

Samson was given the vow of a Nazarite, meaning he was to abstain from any alcohol and keep himself from ritual uncleanness. He was to avoid anything that would deaden his senses or darken his soul. A Nazarite was not to cut his hair. The Nazarite vow could be made for a certain period of time; however, Samson's vow was a lifetime commitment.

While Samson observed some of the outward rules of the Nazarite lifestyle, he never seemed to embrace the purity of character intended to go with this commitment. He did not honor and cherish the high calling God had placed on him. As a young man, Samson rejected the counsel of his parents, hid his doings from them, and pursued his own pleasure.

Nevertheless, God gave Samson superhuman strength and success. But like too many gifted people, Samson grew proud of God's gifts. He began using his strength for his own ends rather than for the pure service of God.

Instead of fleeing from sin at the earliest opportunity as Joseph did, Samson flirted with it. He thought he was strong enough to resist. He thought he could play with fire and not get burned. When he was away from people who knew of his Nazarite calling, he allowed himself to become unclean. Even his attacks on Israel's enemies often displayed more of a desire for personal retaliation than an intent to glorify God.

Samson enjoyed the sense of strength and the thrill of danger he gained by going behind enemy lines and treading on forbidden ground. Attractive and powerful, Samson seemed to believe he was too strong to fall and too tough to flee. He never sought to be accountable to anyone else. Perhaps he thought he could get by with this careless and selfish lifestyle since he was still being used by God.

Samson had an immoral heart, and he was magnetized by immoral women. He loved physical gratification. The attractiveness of a woman could lure him to compromise what he knew was right. Even when he knew a woman was working against him, he refused to flee, thinking he could control her. Samson clung to the pleasures of sin even when they threatened to destroy him. Satan has many strongholds built in the land of compromise.

First, Samson dialogued with temptation; then he entertained it; then he embraced it.

Samson thought he was invincible; others might get caught, but not he. He was wrong. In the end, a woman he thought he loved wore him down with her constant begging until he gave her the secret of his strength. Even as she worked to betray him for money, he followed her like an ox to the slaughter. When God's Spirit left him, Samson did not even notice, but arrogantly went out to fight in his own strength.

In the end, Samson was captured by the Philistines, enslaved, and robbed of his sight. In reality, however, Samson was captured by his own sin. Long before that day, he had already become a slave to his passions and a prisoner of his lusts. Samson lost his physical eyes to the Philistines because he had been spiritually blind to the danger of his sinful life.

Samson fulfilled the proverb, "He that keepeth company with harlots spendeth his substance" (Proverbs 29:3b). When Samson finally came to himself, owned his sin, and cried out to God, he was forgiven and his strength returned; but his final victory over the Philistines cost him his life.

Samson was a poor example of a judge of God's people. God used him to deliver Israel from the Philistines, but he could have been far greater had he subdued his passions and lived a life of honor to God.

‹ Discussing and Pondering ›

Illustration:
Bring a corn kernel and an ear of corn to class. Discuss how the seeds you plant determine what will grow. Look at how the single seed, when planted, multiplies into many more kernels on the ear. Discuss how the crop always comes much later than the planting.

‹ Engaging Yourself— Memorization and Application ›

"Be not deceived; God is not mocked: for whatsoever a man soweth, that shall he also reap. For he that soweth to his flesh shall of the flesh reap corruption; but he that soweth to the Spirit shall of the Spirit reap life everlasting" (Galatians 6:7–8).

Suggested Reading

The Purity Principle, by Randy Alcorn
Not Even a Hint/Sex Is Not the Problem (Lust Is), by Joshua Harris
I Kissed Dating Goodbye, by Joshua Harris
Boy Meets Girl, by Joshua Harris
Passion and Purity, by Elizabeth Elliot
Quest for Love, by Elizabeth Elliot

LESSON 6
Success and Responsibility

‹ Analyzing God's Word ›
Genesis 39:1–6, 21–23; Genesis 41; Genesis 47:13–26

Building Trust

Luke 16:10–12 emphasizes a great truth: one who is faithful in little will be entrusted with much. Joseph did not consider any responsibility insignificant or beneath his dignity—he was faithful in it all! God's smile was on Joseph, for He knew He could trust him.

Joseph placed his confidence in God, and God in turn placed confidence in Joseph. As Joseph practiced faithfulness, he was given more responsibilities.

Joseph's noble life amid ignoble surroundings drew the attention and blessing of God and other people. Like the Lord Jesus centuries later (Luke 2:52), Joseph grew in favor with God and man. Those who watched his exemplary life knew God's hand was on him, and those in authority over him found themselves blessed because of him.

Holding Fast to Integrity

Obedience to parents and others in authority is a sign of high character. Jacob may have favored Joseph because he was the son of his favorite wife, but it seems to have been Joseph's obedience and faithfulness that led his father to trust him with great responsibilities. In giving Joseph the coat of many colors, Jacob seemed to show his intention to treat Joseph as his firstborn. (Jacob's blessings on his sons in Genesis 49 show he weighed character as more important than birth order. At least three brothers disqualified themselves from special blessings and prominent positions in the family because of their wrong actions and lack of integrity.)

Joseph honored his father with his willingness to serve and his determination to do his work completely. When he was given the unpleasant task of checking on the brothers who hated him, he said, "Here I am."

Joseph's father was concerned about the brothers feeding their flocks near Shechem—perhaps because of the enemies Simeon and Levi had made by massacring the men of Shechem a few years earlier. After walking sixty miles, Joseph discovered that his brothers were no longer at Shechem. Yet Joseph left no stone unturned in his dedication to finishing his task. Going beyond his father's specific instructions, Joseph kept looking until he found his brothers at Dothan, ten miles farther on.

After Joseph's father, the next person whom the Scripture records taking special notice of Joseph's character and God's blessing on him was his Egyptian master, Potiphar. Although Joseph had been demoted from favored son to slave, he still served with cheerfulness. Rather than despising his master, he sought to bless him. Joseph knew he would grow by honoring and supporting those over him rather than tearing them down. Joseph paid attention to his surroundings and quickly learned a new language and new tasks.

Joseph's honesty and trustworthiness were probably the

greatest reasons Potiphar chose to promote him to overseer of his estate. Potiphar trusted Joseph so completely that he did not even concern himself with his possessions; only Joseph knew the extent of Potiphar's wealth.

Joseph never demanded this position or felt entitled to it. He carried his master's trust as an honor, not as something he had earned. Not even flattery, temptations of pleasure, or fear of revenge could make him betray the trust of his master or dishonor his God. In spite of the honor he received, Joseph never considered himself above temptation or failure, and he never let down his guard.

No matter who Joseph's human master was, he recognized that God was his ultimate Lord. Joseph was not simply pleasing man, but he was serving the King of heaven and seeking His approval. Joseph sought the "Audience of One."

Holding Fast to God

When the lust of his master's wife turned to jealousy and hate, Joseph found himself knocked down again, and this time he fell even lower—into the dungeon. Did he say, "So much for playing by the rules"? Did Joseph use any means possible to get out? Did he trample others to better himself? Did he plot his revenge on the woman who had lied about him? No, the wrongs done against him did not consume him.

In prison, we see Joseph again serving those around him, and before long he was placed in charge of everything the prisoners did. This is quite an honor for a prisoner charged with attempted rape of an official's wife. Although Joseph now had authority over all the activities of the prison, he still did not create any dissension or try to escape. While he did appeal to the butler to present his case to Pharaoh, he never took things into his own hands or tried to force the issue.

Joseph's former master, Potiphar, was the captain of the guard. The captain of the guard had authority over the keeper of the prison and could have been called the chief executioner of Pharaoh. In other words, Potiphar was in charge of the prison where Joseph was held. He must have been aware of Joseph's behavior in prison and of the position the keeper had given him. When two special cases came before Potiphar—the king's butler and baker—the captain of the guard personally charged Joseph with their care.

Joseph was forgotten in prison for two more years. Even the hope that the butler would remember him seemed to have fallen through. Still we still see him faithfully doing what he was assigned. Unclouded by bitterness  and revenge, Joseph's mind remained sharp and creative, and his heart stayed open to God's direction and blessing. This is why, when he left prison two years later, he was able to envision a solution and a plan of action for Egypt's approaching crisis.

When Pharaoh brought Joseph before him to interpret his ominous dreams, he observed that Joseph's advice was good. Although Joseph was both a prisoner and a foreigner, Pharaoh thought he could not find anyone else like Joseph, who had the Spirit of God in him. He said, "There is none so discreet and wise as thou art" (Genesis 41:39).

Holding Fast to the Dream

Thirteen years after his dream from God that he would someday be a ruler, Joseph, having been faithful through all his trials, was elevated to governor of Egypt. At last his faithfulness was being rewarded!

Overnight, Joseph became a national hero, with power and wealth at his disposal. Yet he did not forget God in his prosperity. Joseph did not credit his own ingenuity, but honored God as the one who had blessed him. He knew God's blessings were not meant for him alone, and he did not hoard them for himself. Joseph saw his new power as a God-given responsibility and an opportunity to save many people's lives.

In carrying out his new responsibilities, Joseph did not lord it over others. He had not trampled others to get to the top, and he would not crush them to maintain his power. Joseph governed with fairness and a caring heart. He did not hand out grain for free, but he ensured that people had a way to earn it. When people's money failed, Joseph did not charge exorbitant interest or seek to build himself up at their expense. When they sold themselves to Pharaoh for food, Joseph promised that when good times returned, they would only owe one-fifth of all they earned—the same rate they had paid while storing grain in preparation for the famine. They considered this more than fair, since Joseph had saved their very lives.

We never see Joseph gloating at his triumph over his brothers, either. He had already forgiven them, recognizing that God was the one directing his life. Both his slavery and his promotion were for his family's salvation.

‹ Comparing Scripture with Scripture ›

You are ready to take leadership responsibility only when God determines that you have learned the lessons you will need to serve with wisdom and gentleness. Readiness for leadership is not based on age but on maturity of character. Even when we think we are ready, we do well to wait on God's direction and timing. 1 Timothy 3:6 cautions against appointing church leaders who are young in age or new Christians, because such men face a great temptation to pride.

If you want to be found faithful and be rewarded with greater responsibility, you must commit to being diligent in menial and boring tasks. Preparation for greater responsibility requires work, study, and character growth.

The most important source of wisdom to study is the Bible. It teaches how to live well, how to please God, and "all things that pertain unto life and godliness" (2 Peter 1:3). The Bible shows how to handle stress and how to lead others effectively.

A New Testament example of someone who maintained his internal focus and his values regardless of circumstances is the Apostle Paul. Paul stated that he had learned how to handle hunger and suffering as well as abundance, fullness, and prosperity (Philippians 4:11–13). The triumphs of life can be even more dangerous than the trials, but a godly person can handle the gifts of God with grace. Paul knew God was the one to whom he would ultimately give account, and his greatest desire was to receive the reward of God's approval.

People who are mature, like Joseph and Paul, can maintain their internal focus and values regardless of their circumstances. While we must beware of the traps of wealth and status, poverty is no guarantee of spirituality. Paul said he could handle hunger and suffering, but also abundance, fullness, and prosperity. He understood that the blessings of God were to be used for God's glory, not to squander on himself.

‹ Discussing and Pondering ›

Should getting ahead socially or gaining wealth be the goal of your life? What if you do gain one of these coveted goals? Will you be satisfied? Many people who have "succeeded" in the worldly sense have found themselves deeply lonely and dissatisfied, and some have even committed suicide.

Why has God placed you in a land of plenty and given you strength, intelligence, health, money, and a home? Have you considered that God has given you these gifts to bless and help others? He does not want you to waste them on yourself. Rather, you are called to protect the weak, lift the lowly, encourage the downtrodden, and care for the poor and abused. Never use your gifts to trample others.

How can you guard your life from being consumed by the love of riches? Think about 1 Timothy 6:10–11, 17–19. Do not love this world's goods, but pursue righteousness, godliness, faith, love, patience, and meekness. Do good and give. This is how you break the grasp of riches on your heart. Keep your focus on what lasts for eternity.

Illustration:

Imagine that you have been given $25,550 to spend as you wish, but that you will never receive any more. How would you spend the money? Now insert *days* in place of *dollars*. 25,550 is the number of days you have if you live to be 70 years old. Are you making the most of the gifts and time you have, or are you wasting them? Can you be trusted with more?

‹ Engaging Yourself— Memorization and Application ›
Work Habits for Success
- Promptness
- Diligence
- Cheerfulness
- Willingness to learn
- Openness to entreaty
- Listening
- Obedience (even if you have a better idea)
- Kindness toward others
- Respect (Don't waste or steal your employer's time or tools.)
- Honesty
- Thriftiness
- Building up your superiors
- Encouraging and lifting up those below you in rank
- Striving to please God

Suggested Reading

Safely Home, by Randy Alcorn (This novel is the story of two men with two measures of success. It also depicts the plight of persecuted Christians in China.)

Where Has Integrity Gone? by Simon Schrock (This book looks at issues of honesty and lying.)

LESSON 7

Preparing for Famine

‹ Analyzing God's Word ›
Genesis 40:20–41:57

The king's butler was released from prison, according to his dream and Joseph's interpretation, but for two years he forgot about Joseph, who was languishing in prison.

Then the king of Egypt had some disturbing dreams. In his dreams he saw seven weak, scrawny cattle devouring seven healthy, vigorous ones, yet the scrawny cattle remained only bags of bones. He saw seven shriveled ears of corn overcome seven plump, full ears, yet the shriveled ears remained wasted. No one could tell him what these dreams meant.

Finally, the butler remembered Joseph in prison. Referring to Joseph not as a prisoner, but as a servant to the captain of the guard, the butler suggested that Pharaoh consult him about the dreams. Immediately Pharaoh summoned Joseph to appear before him.

Pharaoh said, "I have heard that you can interpret dreams."

Joseph realized that his reputation had reached the palace itself, but he refused to take credit for his wisdom. Instead he deflected the praise to where it belonged, replying, "It is not in me: God shall give Pharaoh an answer of peace" (Genesis 41:16).

God did show Joseph the meaning of the two dreams. There were seven years of plenty coming, followed by seven years of famine. The double dream was meant to make clear that the events predicted were a certainty.

Joseph could have used this opportunity to bargain with Pharaoh for his own freedom, but he seems not even to have mentioned his desire for release from prison. He had learned God's power on behalf of the humble and patient, and he knew that now was not the time to seek his own wellbeing.

A Wise Plan

With the future of Egypt at stake, Joseph realized that critical preparations should be made immediately. He suggested that Pharaoh appoint someone trustworthy to prepare for the famine by storing the surpluses from the years of plenty. His plan included storing enough for all Egypt and surrounding nations.

In assessing the situation and recommending a response, Joseph was not campaigning for the job. He was simply pointing out that in handling the distribution of grain, the right man could be a deliverer, while the wrong man could be a tyrant.[35]

Joseph recommended that preparations begin promptly. He did not say, "We have seven years to enjoy before we prepare." Many people have a tendency to spend or waste whatever surplus they have. Without careful saving, they do not have abundance even if they

have times of great prosperity. The seven years of plenty would have done Egypt no good in the coming famine without wise management of the surplus grain.

Righteousness Rewarded

Pharaoh and his court recognized that Joseph's interpretation of the dream was correct. They were impressed by his wisdom and could see that the Spirit of God was in him. Pharaoh declared, "There is none so discreet and wise as thou art" (Genesis 41:39). Pharaoh knew they could find no one else who was directed by God as Joseph was. What better man to carry out Joseph's plan?

In a matter of minutes, Joseph went from a slave and prisoner to a ruler. Only Pharaoh himself would be greater. Joseph was given the use of a royal chariot, dressed in royal attire, and offered the opportunity to marry a prominent woman. He was given a new name meaning "revealer of secrets." Pharaoh commanded everyone to bow before Joseph.

Joseph had no time to revel in the glory of his position. Instead, he began implementing his plan. He went through the land and established storehouses. During the years of plenty, he gathered one-fifth of the abundant harvest—corn "as the sand of the sea," so much that he finally stopped counting it. Was it really necessary to gather so much?

As Joseph had predicted, the famine came, and the people were shocked at its severity. Pharaoh sent everyone in need to Joseph, and Joseph sold them grain to sustain their lives. If anyone had doubted his wisdom before, they now regarded him as the savior of the land.

This famine did not affect Egypt alone; it was severe in the whole region. The Bible says "all countries" came to Egypt for Joseph's aid. Even his own family came from Canaan.

‹ Comparing Scripture with Scripture ›

1 Peter 1:4 says our inheritance is incorruptible, undefiled, and unfading.

In Matthew 6:19–21, Jesus says our hearts follow where we store our treasure. If you want to have your heart and mind on the things of God, invest your time and resources in His kingdom. Do you give God the best of your time and earnings?

If you want to develop a heart for missions, begin by giving to a mission, and you will soon grow interested in the work of that mission. Investing in prayer is also a key way to put your heart in the right place. Too often we sit around waiting for the right feelings before we act, and Satan will do all he can to keep you from feeling motivated. Faith acts based on fact, and the feelings follow.

Financial Responsibility

Following are some ways to live a life of financial freedom and responsibility:

Live Debt-Free

- Save up for a purchase rather than putting it on a credit card. We should not foolishly take on debt. "The borrower is servant to the lender" (Proverbs 22:7). The devil has made many people unavailable for service because of their debt. Don't let your present lusts for things you "must" have become a chain that will tie you down. Forgoing immediate gratification builds character.
- If you do have debts, be honorable and pay what you owe. Be a person of your word. Pay your bills or work out a plan to do so.

Live Within Your Means

- Spend less than you make, not the other way around.

Spend Wisely

- Pray about things you are considering buying. Ask yourself, "Is this a need or a want? How long will this last? Does this fit into God's plan for my life?" Think about the majority of people who do not have the luxury you may be contemplating. Do you really need it? God does not call us to live the "American Dream." Are you a responsible spender?

Care for What God Has Given You
- If you are in charge of the care of a family or employees, seek to meet their needs.
- Do not be wasteful. While we should not worship our things or value them above relationships and eternal values, we should take care of the resources we have. We live in a throw-away society, and many of us have developed a cheap outlook on life and have lost the art of taking care of our things. Why would God give you more to care for if you trash or waste what He has already given you?
- How do you handle unexpected good fortune (blessings) and responsibilities?

Be a Steward of Others' Possessions
- We are not to live as if our lives are all about us. Everything we have is on loan from God, and we will give account for how we use it.
- Do you find it easy to spend another's wealth? Some people believe it is okay for them to take advantage of their employer since the boss has more than they do. They feel that it is their right to take from those over them since they "will not miss the extra" or "do not need it." If you think it is okay to take or destroy someone else's possessions, consider how that will affect others who also depend on him for a job or care. Are you envious of others over you? Can you carefully use and honor another's possessions when you are entrusted with them?

Give to the Kingdom of God
- Give regularly to God and His kingdom (1 Corinthians 16:2). How much should we give? Tithes (10 percent of income) and offerings can reflect a heart that is dedicated to God, but they are not a proof of godliness. God does not limit our giving to 10 percent. Go beyond that amount. The tithe required in the Old Testament was designed to remind us that all of our assets belong to God. (Malachi 3:8–11 encourages us to not cheat God, but to put Him first. In the New Testament, Jesus does not limit our giving to 10 percent, but challenges us to give freely out of love for God and compassion for others.)
- To give your tithe and then believe that the rest is yours to squander or indulge yourself with clearly shows where your heart is. Where you put your money shows what you worship and treasure (Matthew 6:20).
- Give joyfully! God's kingdom is the only secure investment. As a Christian, your challenge is to see how much you can give, not how little you can give and get by.

Pay Your Taxes
- This is a command of God and is not contingent on a government that uses the money wisely. Paying taxes reflects our honor and obedience to earthly authorities and to God.

‹ Discussing and Pondering ›
Preparing for Tough Times

Read, Study, and Memorize Scripture
Build on an eternal foundation and wean yourself from the things of this world. Learn to live with less. In the USA, we are privileged with the opportunity to own, read, and study God's Word. The level of freedom we have is rare and fragile. Are we preparing for a time when it could be taken away?

How do we store up for times of spiritual famine—a famine of God's Word? Are we hiding it in our hearts? Are we storing it up while it is available? How would you survive if your Bible were taken away?

Build a Life of Character
Stability of character and confidence in God will get you through. Treasure laid up in heaven is a secure investment. Matthew 6:25–34 gives us guidance on the kind of pursuits that should consume our time.

Provide for your own family both physically and spiritually. We must pass on a legacy to our children, and treasures of character and spirit are the most important. Proverbs 20:7 says integrity brings a blessing on our children. How do we build a vision and faith for future generations?

Invest in People

People are eternal beings. See how many you can influence or encourage to be part of God's kingdom. Eternal souls are a secure investment in heaven.

How do we prepare for the possible bankruptcy or social collapse of our nation? Storing up wealth or food will not get you through the hard times. We must build reliance upon God, the one who can take us through any trial.

A Handout or a Hand Up?

Was Joseph selfishly accumulating wealth at the expense of the people? No, he understood that just giving it away could have created selfishness, greed, and ungratefulness among the people. By selling it at a fair price, Joseph built respect for the value of what they received. People appreciate better what they have earned or worked for—not what is just handed to them.

Joseph did not take advantage of the people in a desperate situation. When he agreed to buy their cattle, land, and persons, he did not make them into worthless slaves. He required only as much as he did before the famine began—20 percent of all their harvest. The Egyptians seem to have considered this a fair decision and praised Joseph for saving their lives. The selling of their lands and lives was not demanded by Joseph, but proposed by the people.

While God blesses those who give, often the best gift is to enable others to reach their objective themselves.

‹ Engaging Yourself— Memorization and Application ›

"Casting all your care upon him; for he careth for you" (1 Peter 5:7).

Additional activity:
Consider a service opportunity or a need you could share with. You may choose a local service project or support something abroad, such as a mission program that not only meets physical needs but gives high priority to teaching the Word of God. Consider why God has given you the talents, gifts, and resources He has.

Suggested Reading

The Other Side of the Wall, by Gary Miller (how to give responsibly to the poor)
The Treasure Principle, by Randy Alcorn
Money, Possessions, & Eternity, by Randy Alcorn
In Light of Eternity, by Randy Alcorn
Radical, by David Platt
Against the Wind, by K.P. Yohannan
The Road to Reality, by K.P. Yohannan

LESSON 8

Joseph Tests His Brothers

‹ Analyzing God's Word ›
Genesis 42–44

When Joseph met his brothers, he had spent more than half of the previous twenty years as a slave and a prisoner. Yet he had been free in heart all the time, neither shackled by hate nor bound by bitterness. His confidence and trust in the sovereignty of God had allowed him to live boldly, without fear.

Godly Wisdom

Why did Joseph keep his identity secret from his brothers, imprison them as national spies, accuse them of stealing, and speak roughly to them when they came to buy grain? Was he finally taking revenge by giving them a taste of their own medicine?

No. Rather, it was great wisdom that caused Joseph to hide his real emotions from his brothers. The easy response would have been to seize this opportunity to attack them for what they had done to him. However, Joseph neither beat them down as soon as they were under his power, nor did he introduce himself and offer forgiveness. Why did he pause and test them so thoroughly?

Joseph had self-control, and he carefully considered the situation before responding to it. As he observed his brothers, he did not judge them, assuming they were the same hateful men they had been twenty years before. Joseph believed God had been working in their hearts. He would test them to see what kind of men they were now.

It was simple for Joseph to appear strange to his brothers; they remembered him as he was twenty years before. Then he had been a defenseless teenager, crying for mercy when they sold him as a slave, and they likely assumed he had long since died.

The Legend

Little did Joseph's brothers know he was now second in command to the king, revered and loved by all the people. His very name, Zaphnath-paaneah, implied that he was a "revealer of secrets" or "savior of the land." Joseph's power to know the future and his prediction of the years of plenty and famine would have been legendary by now. Everyone knew the immense storehouses of grain were the work of Zaphnath-paaneah.

All these stories were likely told to Joseph's brothers when they came into Egypt. They bowed before the powerful governor, who in their minds was an Egyptian. They assumed he could not understand their language, since he spoke to them through an interpreter.

The Tables Had Turned

Did Joseph gloat over them? Did he seek to remind them that his dreams had come true after all? No, he tested them. Were they still the same hateful men? Twenty years before, they had betrayed their favored brother to a life of slavery and condemned their father to sorrow. Would they do it again if they had the chance? Had they learned their lesson?

Joseph sternly accused his brothers of being national spies and put them into prison. However, he provided a way for them to prove their "innocence"—they must bring their youngest brother to Egypt as proof of their story. As trouble began to fall on them, Joseph's brothers immediately assumed God was judging them for the way they had treated Joseph long ago. When Joseph overheard their conversation, he turned away and wept. His heart was full of love, yet the test was not over—what was their attitude toward his younger brother Benjamin? Were they still jealous and envious?

Testing

Choosing Simeon to stay behind in prison as insurance that the brothers would return, Joseph sent the others home with food for their families. He instructed his steward to return their money to their sacks. (Later the steward told the brothers he had received their money. Did Joseph give it out of his own pocket?) This was a test of the brothers' honesty. The Bible says their "hearts failed them" when they found it, and once again they assumed God was judging them.

At first, Jacob refused to let the brothers take Benjamin to Egypt, but he relented after Judah promised to be responsible for Benjamin's safety. The brothers returned to Egypt with Benjamin, and again they fulfilled the dreams of Joseph by bowing before him.

Now Joseph gave his brothers a new test: he took them to his home to dine as guests. The brothers were afraid to be brought to his home, but they were reassured when Simeon was released from prison and reunited with them. Joseph maintained his persona of mystery and knowledge by seating his brothers according to their ages. Since these men were in their forties, this was an incredible feat for someone outside the family, and the brothers wondered at the extraordinary wisdom of the strange ruler.

Joseph also used the feast as an opportunity to see if his brothers were prone to jealousy toward Benjamin. Knowing that Benjamin was now the favorite son of his father, Joseph showered him with extra privileges. He gave Benjamin five times as much food as his brothers. They did not appear jealous, but the test was not over.

The next morning Joseph again ordered his steward to return the brothers' payments to their sacks of grain—and also to hide the governor's special silver cup in Benjamin's sack. After the brothers had left, Joseph's steward overtook them and accused them of returning evil for good. Playing up Joseph's reputation for supernatural abilities, the steward scolded the brothers for being foolish enough to steal from Zaphnath-paaneah. (Later, when they were brought before Joseph, he asked them, "Wot ye not [don't you know] that such a man as I can certainly divine?" [Genesis 44:15].)

Knowing they had not taken the cup, the brothers agreed that if any of them were found with the cup, he would become the governor's slave. What a shock they had when the cup was found in Benjamin's sack! This final test would reveal how loyal they were to their favored brother. Joseph assured them that since the cup was in Benjamin's sack, they could all go home—only Benjamin must stay as a slave. Were the brothers looking for an opportunity to get rid of Benjamin as they had Joseph?

Passing the Test

Years before, Joseph's brothers thought nothing of destroying the brother they despised and bringing grief to their father. On this day, however, they all returned and offered themselves as slaves in exchange for their privileged youngest brother. By doing so, they showed both compassion for Benjamin and honor toward their father. Judah, especially, showed a change of attitude toward Benjamin.

As the brothers bowed before Joseph to plead for mercy, they revealed once again the guilt they had been living under all those years. They told Joseph, "God hath found out the iniquity of thy servants." It seems that the guilt of what they had done to Joseph and the fear of being discovered had haunted them all those years.

Judah explained to Joseph how he had become a

pledge for Benjamin, and how his father would die if Benjamin did not return—and Judah himself would bear the blame. "Let me stay instead," he pleaded. Judah, an ancestor of Jesus, offered himself as a substitute for his condemned brother, as Jesus would later offer Himself for us.

Joseph's brothers had passed all the tests, and Joseph knew they wanted to be free from the lies and wickedness of their past. He could contain himself no longer, and he finally revealed himself to his brothers. After a tearful reunion, Joseph sent them home again, this time with instructions to return with his father and all their families.

‹ Building Your Word Knowledge ›
Seeking or Doubting

God delights in proving Himself to those who seek Him, but constantly questioning or challenging His character insults His patience and goodness. The difference between honest seeking and unbelieving doubt lies in the attitude of the heart. Some people question God in order to understand what God is doing or what He wants, as Mary did in Luke 1:34. Others question God in a way that challenges and questions His character. They may doubt God's character or His ability, as Zacharias seems to have done in Luke 1:18. God was pleased with Mary's response, but Zacharias was judged for unbelief.

On the other hand, we *should* test others to learn whether their claims are genuine and whether they are teaching the truth. We may also test others to help them think through what they believe. This is the kind of constructive testing Jesus and Joseph did.

‹ Comparing Scripture with Scripture ›
Healing Relationships with Wisdom

True godly sorrow for sins against others includes a sincere admission of fault—"I am sorry, I have sinned," not, "I am sorry *if I hurt you*." However, godly sorrow is more than just saying you're sorry.

Godly sorrow includes taking time to consider the pain your wrongdoing has caused someone else. It means grieving for what you did to the other, not merely being sorry you got caught.

Repentance includes making things right to the best of your ability. For example, if you have stolen from someone, pay back what you have taken. Sometimes full healing only comes as we make restitution for what we've done wrong.

Repentance and Consequences

Just because you have repented of something and left it in the past does not mean there will be no consequences. For example, Matthew 18:32–35 implies that if we refuse to forgive others, God will hold us accountable for our own debts, even if they had already been forgiven.

God's forgiveness does not erase all the lasting effects of what we've done. Furthermore, being forgiven by others does not immediately restore the relationship. Trust that has been broken must be earned again.

‹ Discussing and Pondering ›
True Freedom and True Slavery

Are you truly free? Some of the freest individuals may be those who are bound physically but are free in spirit. People with clean consciences have nothing to hide. The one who confesses his sin finds pardon. The one who releases his hurts to the keeping of God has freedom. Such a person has learned to accept his condition and trust the sovereignty and providence of God in his life.

Just the Way We Are

"God loves us just the way we are!" While this saying is true, people often use it to excuse themselves for continuing to live in sin. Romans 5:6–10 says God loved us while we were in sin. However, He never condones a life of continual sin. Jesus was known as the *friend of sinners*, yet He never made them comfortable with their sin or joined them in it. Rather, He always called them *out* of sin. God shows us His love by setting us *free* from sin.

Illustration:
Some people might consider Joseph cruel for his treatment of his brothers, but consider a butcher knife and a surgeon's scalpel. While both are used for cutting, one brings death and the other brings healing (Proverbs 27:6). Joseph's actions brought healing to his brothers and his family.

Purposes for Punishment

There was a young man who was sentenced for doing something wrong that endangered others. He stood before a judge and received a penalty for his actions. Even though he was sorry, he still received discipline and punishment. The judge felt it was important to administer discipline for the following reasons:

- Discipline corrects the wrongdoer.
- Discipline gives a warning to others.
- Discipline maintains a sense of stability for a community.

‹ Engaging Yourself—Memorization and Application ›
Confronting Others with Wisdom

Below are some considerations and precautions to take if you need to confront someone about wrongdoing in his life:

- Take time to control your emotions and "cool down." Anger causes the conflict to escalate (Proverbs 15:1).
- Prepare yourself with prayer.
- Write down what you plan to say.
- Ask the other person if you have understood the situation correctly. What you saw as an offense may be only a misunderstanding.
- Clear up small things early, and do not allow supposed hurts to grow large in your mind.
- Do not approach someone with an accusing attitude. There are always two sides to a story, and the person you're confronting probably has been hurt too; you may even have contributed to the problem.
- Remember that you could fail in the same way as the person you are approaching (Galatians 6:1).
- Go as a friend. How would you like someone to approach you?
- Depending on how emotionally involved you are in the situation, it may be wise to ask someone else to accompany you to keep you accountable and calm.

"Faithful are the wounds of a friend; but the kisses of an enemy are deceitful" (Proverbs 27:6).

LESSON 9
Revenge or Forgiveness?

‹ Analyzing God's Word ›
Genesis 45, 50

Unexpected Forgiveness

Fear and confusion overwhelmed Joseph's brothers. They expected him to take revenge on them, as most people would have done. They knew they deserved to be punished for the atrocities they had committed against Joseph. When he told them who he was, they were shocked and greatly troubled. They were not expecting what came next. Instead of lashing out in anger, Joseph wept.

We should not be afraid to cry. Tears are a means of healing. Real men can and should show emotions. Jesus Himself wept, and said, "Blessed are they that mourn" (Matthew 5:4). Your heart should be soft enough to weep—especially over the hurts of others.

Joseph called his brothers near, kissed them, and forgave them. They had nothing to be afraid of. He told them, "Now therefore be not grieved, nor angry with yourselves, that ye sold me hither: for God did send me before you to preserve life" (Genesis 45:5). These were not mere words; Joseph sincerely meant them. He was grateful that God had used the tragedies of his life to save many people.

At Peace with God's Plan

Like Joseph, can we see that it is not people but God who directs our lives? Joseph trusted in the fact that his life was ordered by God, not by the actions of others. His stern attitude toward his brothers during their testing concealed a heart that yearned for his brothers to be at peace.

On what basis could Joseph forgive his brothers and do good to them? How could he have such an intense love for them? The source of Joseph's love was the divine love of God that filled his heart. Before being reunited with his brothers, Joseph himself had experienced God's love and forgiveness. When the One who is love is in your heart, there is no room for hate or revenge. Joseph seems to have learned the key to forgiving quickly, for he had clearly forgiven his brothers long before they arrived in Egypt asking for grain.

Forgive Early and Often

Forgiveness is best cultivated when hurts are small. The longer we nurture a grudge, the harder it is for us to release it; it entwines its tentacles all through our hearts. We must choose not to be easily offended. As bakers grease their hands to keep the dough from sticking to them, we must continually "grease our hearts" with prayer and love for others to keep the dough of

bitterness from clinging to us. We must quickly and constantly release our hurts to God.

An Unexpected Hurt

Do you think this sudden revelation was too much for Benjamin? What a shock to find out after twenty years that his brother Joseph had not been killed by a wild animal, but rather had been cruelly treated and sold as a slave by his own brothers! How do you think that must have made Benjamin feel toward his brothers? Benjamin was now faced with a choice between taking up a grudge or forgiving his brothers and releasing his sense of loss to God.

It is easy to take up a grudge for someone else, even if that person has forgiven the wrong. Perhaps we fear that the culprits will get away without consequences. But a secondary grudge, though it may seem less selfish, will only increase the damage caused by the offense. A grudge hurts our relationships even if the original offense was not against us.

Joseph probably wanted Benjamin present for this reunion as a witness that he was actually alive and that he forgave his brothers (Genesis 45:12). He also used Benjamin to test the other brothers for envy.

Unexpected Provision

Joseph did not stop with saying, "I forgive you." He proved his forgiveness with actions of goodness toward his brothers. There were five more years of famine left. Joseph not only forgave his brothers, but he also invited them to come down and live where he could provide for them and their families.

When his brothers left for Canaan to bring their father and families, Joseph warned them not to quarrel on the way. Maybe he feared that they would fall into accusing each other for the parts they had played in Joseph's bondage. Joseph wanted hard feelings and regrets to be put behind them.

Although it must have been hard for the brothers to tell their father the complete truth, it was surely a relief to have everything in the open at last. Full honesty and godly sorrow is essential for complete healing (John 3:20–21).

Seventeen years later, after their father's death, Joseph's brothers were still afraid Joseph would try to get even. They came to Joseph again, asking him to forgive them for their father's sake, and promising, "Behold, we be thy servants" (Genesis 50:18). Joseph had forgiven them long ago, yet they were still living under guilt and fear.

Like salvation, forgiveness is a free gift, but it does you no good until you accept it.

When his brothers came with this appeal, Joseph wept. It hurt to see them doubt his love for them. "Fear not," he said, "for am I in the place of God? But as for you, ye thought evil against me; but God meant it unto good, to bring to pass, as it is this day, to save much people alive" (Genesis 50:19–20). Joseph knew it was not his responsibility to judge his brothers. He saw the big picture God intended—"to save much people alive"— rather than focusing on his personal happiness. Joseph comforted and encouraged his brothers, promising to care for them and their children.

An Unexpected Lifestyle

Revenge and retribution are common human responses to personal injury. It would have been natural for Joseph to have sought to get even with his brothers. Is a response right just because it is expected and normal? No, God's ways are different from those of fallen man, and His will is for us to be like Him.

Joseph's life was patterned after the image and will of God, not after "normal" human behavior. Looking at how he lived, one might think he had been reading the teachings of Jesus, Paul, or John (Matthew 5:38–48; Romans 12:16–21; 1 John 2:7–11). Forgiveness and loving your enemies are usually thought of as New Testament attitudes. Where did Joseph learn these attitudes? We recognize that he was close to God and acted after His character. Jesus said, "Blessed are the peacemakers, for they shall be called the children of God" (Matthew 5:9).

Do we jump at the opportunity for revenge if the tables turn in our favor, or do we forgive those who are undeserving? Will we seek revenge or allow God to repay wrongdoing as He chooses?

Unexpected Faith

God is the only one who can be totally fair in judgment, because He can see the motives and thoughts of the heart. God's payday is not every Friday. In all honesty, would we want God to withhold His mercy or give us exactly what we deserve? (See Ezra 9:13.)

Does faith in the sovereignty of God help us overcome the desire for revenge? Can we say, "What you did to me was part of God's plan"? Can we see the overall guidance of God in our lives?

‹ Building Your Word Knowledge ›

Illustration:

Bring two weeds to class—one small and intact, and one large, with a broken taproot. Explain how bitterness is like the root of a weed; most of it is below the surface, and it is much easier to pull it out of our lives when it is small. Waiting and trying later to dig out established weeds of bitterness causes much more pain than dealing with it promptly.

‹ Discussing and Pondering ›

How Do We Love Our Enemies?

This command demands positive action. God's call takes us beyond what is expected of us. Loving our enemies means not only "cutting them slack," but also actively blessing them by giving them what they do not deserve and heaping love on them.

Forgiveness Is Vital

Why God asks you to forgive:
- God wants *you* to be free.
- God wants you to realize that pain can bring growth in your life.
- God wants to restore the other party; He loves him/her too.
- God's forgiveness of your sins depends on your forgiveness of others.
- Holding onto bitterness will eat at you, causing many health issues that shorten your life.
- God has forgiven you of so much that the wrongs you are called to forgive are minor compared to sins that you have been forgiven of.

- If you keep your hands out of the mess, you allow God to judge fairly.

‹ Engaging Yourself— Memorization and Application ›

An Inconsistency in Joseph's Timeline?

When we read of the genealogy of Moses in Exodus and tally up the ages of each person, it appears that the family's stay in Egypt lasted for a little more than two hundred years (Genesis 46:8, 11; Exodus 6:18, 20; 7:7; the generations from Levi to Moses are listed as Levi, Kohath, Amram, and Moses).

In Henry Morris' book *The Genesis Record,* he records that Jacob's family grew rapidly to nearly one hundred people in the fifty years before they moved to Egypt. This was a growth rate of more than 6 percent a year. Assuming an average 5 percent growth rate throughout their time in Egypt, they could have numbered two million in only 215 years.[36]

How do we reconcile this with the passages in Genesis 15:13–16 and Exodus 12:40–41 that give us a number of 430 years for Israel's time in Egypt? Some scholars point out that some manuscripts of Exodus 12:40 say the sojourning of the children of Israel included the time spent in both Canaan *and* Egypt. Galatians 3:16–18 would seem to confirm this. It states that 430 years passed from the giving of the promise to Abraham to the giving of the Law to Moses.

- From Abraham's entrance into Canaan to the birth of Isaac was 25 years.
- Isaac was 60 at the birth of Jacob.
- Jacob was 130 when he moved to Egypt.
- Jacob and his descendants lived in Egypt for 215 years.
- This makes 430 years altogether.

Living in Egypt for 215 years was still a long time. Consider what can happen in that time. This is only a few years less than the total time the United States has been a nation.

Why Goshen?

Joseph instructed his family to announce that they were

shepherds—a despised profession among Egyptians. To avoid associating with these shepherds, the Egyptians offered to let them live in Egypt's best pastureland undisturbed.

Besides providing for his family's immediate material needs, Joseph was also trying to keep them separate from Egyptian society. This separation enabled them to maintain their pilgrim status and avoid being assimilated into the pagan culture.

The Nile River in Egypt (www.padfield.com)

Joseph was visionary enough to concern himself with Israel's long-term future and permanence as a nation. He knew God had promised Abraham, Isaac, and Jacob that they would inherit the land of Canaan. The blessing on Joseph's family included the promise that the Deliverer of all mankind would arrive through them. Thus, in faith, Joseph promised his family that Egypt would not be their final home. Someday they would return to Canaan.

Are you entangled by the duties of your temporary life (2 Timothy 2:4)? Do you realize that this world is not your home, and that you are just passing through? We are called to be pilgrims and strangers in this present world (Hebrews 11:13–16).

The Close of Joseph's Life

Although Israel (Jacob) was anxious to see his son Joseph again, he may have been uncertain about leaving the land of promise for Egypt. In Genesis 46:1–4, we read that Israel stopped at Beersheba to offer sacrifices and seek God's direction.

God told Israel not to fear: "I will go down with thee into Egypt; and I will also surely bring thee up again" (Genesis 46:4).

Israel lived seventeen years in Egypt. He charged Joseph with burying him in the land promised to him and his fathers (usually the responsibility of the firstborn). Israel gave a special blessing to each of his sons and prophesied their return to Canaan someday. After his death, his sons honored his request and buried him in the burial ground of Abraham and Isaac, but they continued living in Egypt.

At Joseph's death, there was no obvious reason for the Israelites to consider leaving Egypt. They had the favor of Pharaoh and enjoyed the best land; however, they remained resident aliens. Their promised land was Canaan. They did not ultimately belong in Egypt.

When it came time for Joseph's burial, he was embalmed, and his body remained in Egypt. However, he was not buried there. In faith, Joseph had commanded his family to take his bones out of Egypt when they left for the Promised Land.

Time often erases memory. After a few decades, a new Pharaoh arrived on the throne who did not remember or appreciate what Joseph had done to save Egypt. The Israelites were still living separately from the Egyptians. Fearing the growing number of Israelites, this Pharaoh oppressed and enslaved them.

Almost 145 years after Joseph's death, Moses led the children of Israel out of Egypt, taking Joseph's bones with them.

After spending more than forty years wandering in the wilderness, the Israelites finally buried Joseph at Shechem in the land of Canaan (Joshua 24:32). The burial site was where Abraham had built his first altar in Canaan after receiving God's promise, "Unto thy seed will I give this land" (Genesis 12:6–7). Perhaps this was the same parcel of ground Jacob had bought as his claim to the land when he returned from his exile in Haran (Genesis 33:19). Shechem/Sychar is the parcel of ground that Jacob gave Joseph (John 4:5–6). It remained within the inheritance given to Ephraim.

Suggested Reading

The Captive, by Christoph Von Schmid (available from Lamplighter Rare Books)

Light Force, by Brother Andrew and Al Janssen (love and peace in the Middle East)

LESSON 10
Jesus: Deliverer for Mankind

‹ Analyzing God's Word ›
The Red Ribbon of His-Story

A Perfect World
God created the world perfect. In the beginning there was no sin or shame to mar the world's beauty or the perfect harmony between God and man. However, this perfection did not last.

Lucifer was one of God's highest created spirits. After he became proud and tried to usurp God's throne, he was thrown out of heaven and became the one we know as Satan. In his rebellion, Satan tried to destroy God's perfect world by corrupting the crowning jewel of His creation—humanity.

A Disaster
God gave mankind a test of obedience—would Adam and Eve believe God, or would they listen to Satan's lies? Adam and Eve were deceived in thinking they were smart enough to decide whom they could trust. By choosing to disobey the Creator, they brought a curse on all mankind and the whole creation. This fall from perfection happened because of human rebellion, in choosing their own way instead of God's commands.

The sin of rebellion spread like a cancer to all Adam's descendants. There is no adult who has not rebelled against God. All have sinned and fallen far short of God's perfection. Our best efforts to do right in our own strength are filthy next to the holiness of our righteous God (Romans 3:23; Isaiah 64:6).

God said that to disobey would bring death. "The wages of sin is death" (Romans 6:23). It is what we earned and deserved. Each of us is guilty, for each of us has inherited this curse and has sinned. Ezekiel 18:20 declares, "The soul that sinneth, it shall die."

100 Percent Obedience Required
We cannot measure up to God's standards by keeping 90 percent of His commands. The law declares that the breaking of only one command makes us sinners before God (James 2:10; Romans 3:19–20).

It is as if we are hanging over a precipice by a chain. Only one link needs to be broken for us to fall.

None of us has the power to escape the sentence of sickness and death brought into the world by sin. Included in this sentence is separation from the presence of God. Sin is not compatible with a holy God. When humans chose to rebel against God, they became subject to God's judgment on the devil and his demons—eternal punishment in hell.

A Perfect Plan
However, God's plan could not be foiled by human weakness or Satan's schemes. God loved the world enough that He made a way to restore our relationship with Him. Immediately after the Fall, God promised that someday He would provide a Deliverer to save us from the curse.

In Genesis 3:15, God promised that the seed of the

woman would someday crush the head of the serpent—that is, Someone descended from Eve would destroy the work of Satan and reverse the curse of sin. Who could this be? It had to be someone who had experienced our curse, but who was not tainted by sin. This might seem like a contradiction, but what is impossible with man is possible with God.

Throughout the Bible we find many glimpses of this coming Deliverer. Until the time of His coming, God provided ways for people to express faith in His provision. This is the purpose of all the sacrifices in the Old Testament—they were acts of faith and trust in the provision of God, foreshadowing the Perfect Sacrifice.

When God killed the first animal to make clothing of skins for Adam and Eve, this was the first time blood was shed because of man's sin. This illustrated the principle of a perfect life given in exchange for a sinful life. The blood of an animal could never take away sin, but when man sacrificed a clean, innocent animal, his sin was covered because he was placing his trust in the coming Deliverer.

The evil disease of sin continued to spread and ferment until the thoughts of man were "only evil continually" (Genesis 6:5). Sin must be judged, so God destroyed the world and all mankind with a worldwide flood, but He preserved the human race and the promise of the Redeemer when He saved Noah and his family, with representatives of each animal kind, in the ark. By providing the ark as the only means of salvation, God painted another illustration of the salvation He would bring through Christ.

Even though the human race started over in a sense, humans remained sinners under the curse of sin and death. Most of humanity still insisted on living in rebellion. Sin still separated man from a holy God. Animal sacrifices were still necessary until the Deliverer would come as the perfect sacrifice. Those who offered sacrifices in faith were coming to God His way.

God gave another picture of the coming Deliverer through a test He gave Abraham. After miraculously giving Abraham and Sarah a son, Isaac, God asked Abraham to sacrifice the promised son as a burnt offering. Surely Abraham must have wondered why God would ask him to slay the very son through whom He promised to bless all nations of the world. Nevertheless, Abraham trusted and obeyed God, and at the last moment God stopped him and provided a ram as a sacrifice in Isaac's place. This ram foreshadowed Christ's death in our place.

As we follow the descendants of Isaac, we see that God used Joseph, Isaac's grandson, to save the family of Israel and preserve the line through which God's promises would come by delivering them from famine and bringing them to Egypt. However, it was Joseph's brother Judah whom God chose to carry the line of the promised Seed (1 Chronicles 5:1–2; Psalm 78:67–68).

At his death, Joseph promised his family that they would return to the land of promise. Satan tried to foil God's plan by making the Israelites slaves in Egypt and inciting Pharaoh to try to destroy the male children.

Then God sent another man, Moses, to represent the coming Deliverer by leading Israel out of Egypt. When Pharaoh refused to let Israel go, God passed through the land and killed all the firstborn males of Egypt. However, God provided a way of escape for Israel from the judgment on Egypt through applying the blood of a lamb to their doorposts. Seeing their obedience and trust in God, the angel of death passed over the homes with the blood. After losing his firstborn, Pharaoh finally drove the Israelites out of Egypt.

Over the following years, God prescribed a detailed system of sacrifices as pictures of the coming Deliverer's sacrifice for sin. A tabernacle was set up as the only place for the people to approach God. A thick veil separating the Holiest Place from the rest of the tabernacle reminded people that sinful humans cannot approach a holy God. The sacrifices of lambs, goats, and cattle seem harsh to us, but God told Israel that their sin could be taken away only through the shedding of blood. The life is in the blood, and the shedding of blood symbolizes the giving of another life in our place (Leviticus 17:11).

As the Israelites traveled through the wilderness during their forty years of wandering, they often complained and rebelled against God. On one of these occasions, God sent poisonous snakes into the camp as a judgment for their complaining, and many died from the bites of the snakes. However, when the people repented and cried out to God for help, God told Moses to make a brass snake and put it on a pole. Everyone who looked at the snake on the pole was healed. Centuries later, the Deliverer, Jesus Himself, referred to this story, saying that just as Moses lifted up the snake in the wilderness, Christ would be lifted up to heal the world.

A Perfect Deliverer

As the time approached for the coming of the Deliverer, God continued to unveil His plan. The Deliverer would be a man to take man's sin, but He would be God as well. God planted His life in the womb of a virgin to bring forth Jesus—the beloved Son of God. Jesus is the eternal God (Luke 1:31–35; Matthew 1:18–23; Isaiah 9:6–7; John 1:1–3, 14–15; John 19:7–9; Revelation 1:8; 4:8; 11:17).

Suddenly, the plan became clear. One of the ancient prophecies stated that the Deliverer would be called Emmanuel—God with us! Only God is perfect, and only He can redeem us.

God became one of us to take away our curse. He was tempted as we are, yet He never sinned (Galatians 3:13; Hebrews 2:14–18).

Jesus, the Deliverer, was betrayed by a friend, sold for money, abandoned, falsely accused, and crucified. He gave Himself as a sacrifice in our place (2 Corinthians 5:21). The Saviour of the world became the perfect sacrificial Lamb, delivering His people through His death. His life was not taken away; He gave it freely. This innocent, divine life was the final, complete sacrifice for sin—the only sacrifice that truly takes away sin (Hebrews 10:1–4, 11–12). God gave Himself for sinners—what great love!

Even as Jesus was dying, He forgave His enemies (Romans 5:8; Colossians 1:21–22). When He died, Jesus cried, "It is finished!" The promise was kept—the Deliverer had come!

When Jesus died, the veil in the temple was torn in half from top to bottom. God had accepted the sacrifice. Now there is a way for man to come into God's presence, past the veil of separation, through the substitution of Jesus.

The greatest evidence that God accepted this sacrifice for sin was the resurrection of Jesus. Only His sacrifice was enough to remove sin, and only He came back to life. None of the animals sacrificed came to life again, even though their blood covered the repentant and believing sinner (Acts 17:31; 1 Corinthians 15:17). God was pleased with Jesus' sacrifice. Jesus' death met the demands of justice; therefore no other sacrifice is needed.

The sacrifice of Jesus takes away our sin. Jesus Christ, the Deliverer, paid the price of our redemption! God accepted Christ's sacrifice for man's sin. Man does not need to die.

Death could not destroy the Son of God, and God raised Him from the dead. Having conquered death forever, Jesus is now seated at God's right hand.

Will you reject the gift of God and insist on trying to come to Him on your own terms? There is only one way to God! We can never pay the price of our sin. The priceless gift of God's favor can never be bought or earned. What must we do? We must accept God's provision and allow Him to change us.

We have been purchased with a great price—the lifeblood of God, and we belong to Him (1 Corinthians 6:19–20; 1 Peter 1:18–19).

When we take Jesus as our Saviour, we must also make Him our Lord. We give up our rebellion and turn from our sin, dying to our old life and surrendering to God. When we come to God this way, He restores us to life through the new birth. Just as our Deliverer rose from the dead to live forever, so we are called to live the new life with Him.

‹ Building Your Word Knowledge ›
"Taking Our Necks Out"

Some missionaries who translated the Bible into a tribal language were puzzled at how to translate the word *redeemer*. After considering the culture of the people for whom they were translating, they settled on the phrase "one who took our necks out."

This word picture drew on the people's experience of seeing lines of slaves tied together with ropes around their necks. On occasion another person would redeem one of them by paying the traders the asking price. Then the rope around the prisoner's neck was released, and his neck was "taken out."

‹ Comparing Scripture with Scripture ›
Hitting the Mark

People often imagine that they can come close to meeting God's standard of righteousness in their own strength, but God's standard is far beyond anything we can do in our own efforts. Suppose you throw a stone at a tree from thirty yards and miss it. You could say you were "close," because you did have a chance of hitting it. Then suppose you stand at the top of a mountain and try to throw a stone across a river in the valley below. Though it may look easy, the river may actually be half a mile away, and you cannot come close to getting a stone to the other side. So it is with human effort. Though we may tell ourselves we "just missed the mark," we are doomed to total failure without God's empowering grace. Fallen humans cannot meet God's requirements (Romans 3:23; Isaiah 64:6).

Illustration:
Take a doll or toy person and tie it to a string with ten knots representing the Ten Commandments. With scissors, cut the string at any knot to let the doll fall. This illustrates James 2:10–11. We do not need to break all or most of God's law to become a transgressor and need repentance.

‹ Discussing and Pondering ›
Missing Heaven by Eighteen Inches

Eighteen inches is about the distance between your head and your heart. There are many people who know about God and say they believe in Jesus, yet have never experienced true faith in their hearts. What they know makes no difference in their lives. Scripture says even the devils believe and tremble (James 2:19). You can know all *about* God without really knowing Him.

‹ Engaging Yourself— Memorization and Application ›

"Now unto him that is able to keep you from falling, and to present you faultless before the presence of his glory with exceeding joy, to the only wise God our Saviour, be glory and majesty, dominion and power, both now and ever. Amen" (Jude 1:24–25).

Suggested Reading

The Stranger on the Road to Emmaus, by John R. Cross, New Tribes Missions

Born Crucified, by L. E. Maxwell

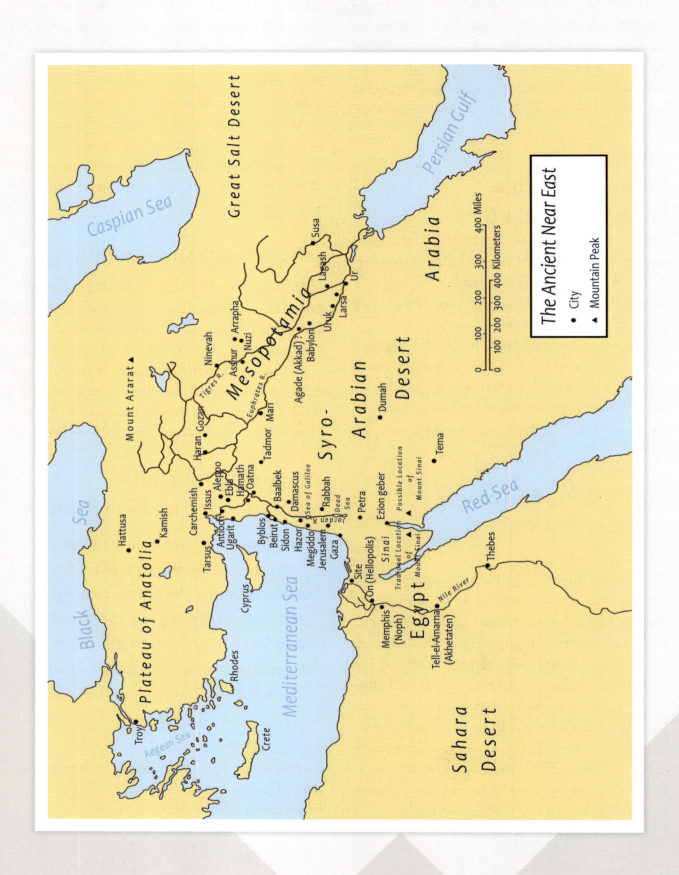

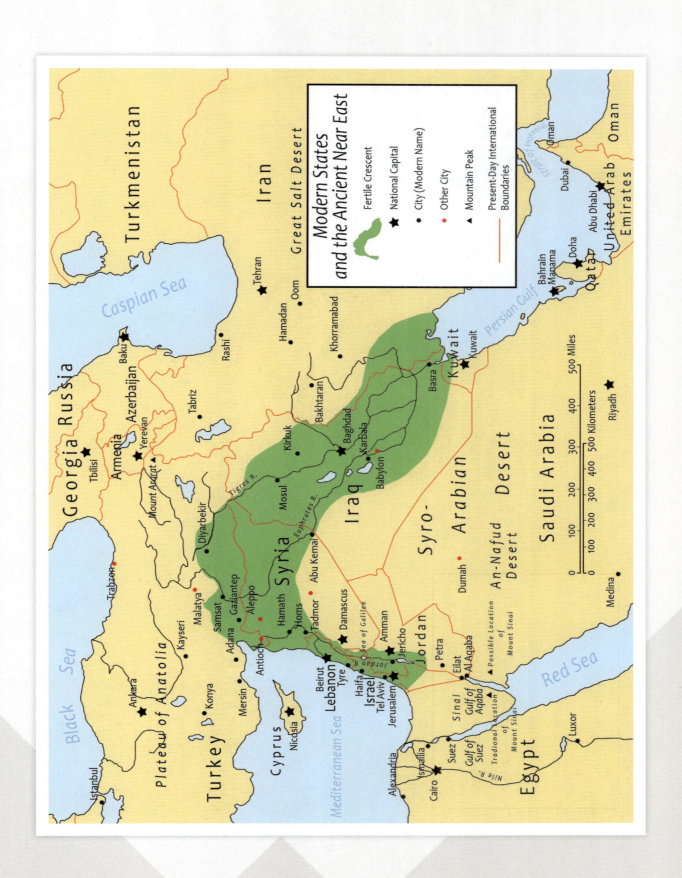

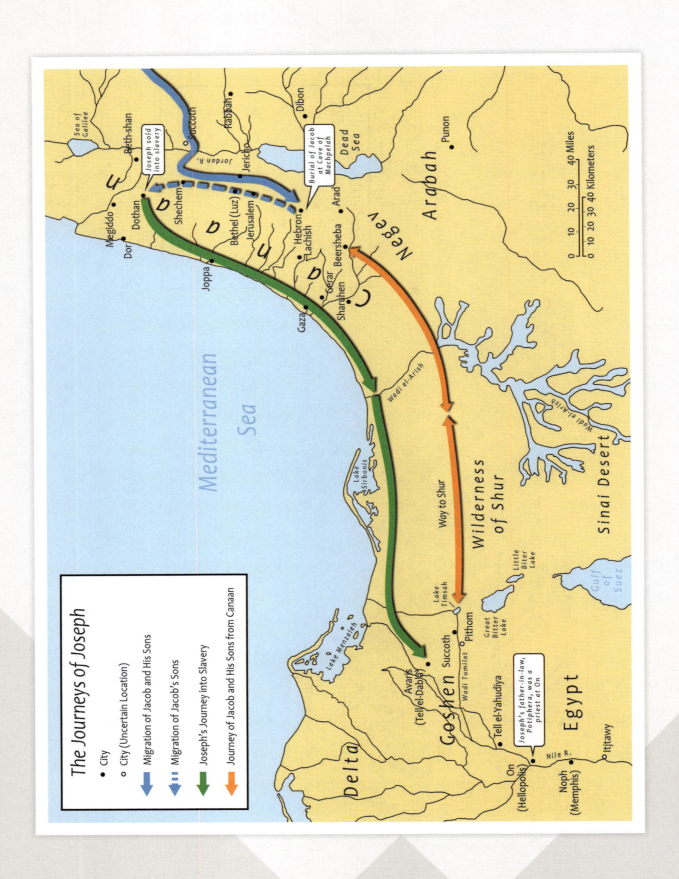

ENDNOTES

1. Institute in Basic Life Principles, Inc., *Character Sketches,* Vol. 1, Institute of Basic Life Principles,Inc.,USA, 1976, p. 273.
2. Mayo Clinic Staff, "Forgiveness: Letting go of grudges and bitterness," Nov. 11, 2014, <http://www.mayoclinic.org/healthy-living/adult-health/in-depth/forgiveness/art-20047692>, accessed January 20, 2015.
3. Gary Smalley and John Trent, *The Gift of the Blessing/The Gift of Honor,* Inspirational Press, New York, 1998, pp. 307–308.
4. Josh Harris, *I Kissed Dating Goodbye,* Multnomah Publishers, Inc., Sisters, OR, 1997, p. 88.
5. Josh Harris, *Boy Meets Girl,* Multnomah Publishers, Inc., Sisters, OR, 2000, p. 153.
6. Ibid., p. 156.
7. Josh Harris, *Sex Is Not the Problem (Lust Is),* Multnomah Publishers, Inc., Sisters, OR, 2003, p. 119.
8. Ibid., p. 73.
9. Josh Harris, *Boy Meets Girl,* p. 164.
10. Lisa Bevere, *Kissed the Girls and Made Them Cry,* Thomas Nelson Publishers, Nashville, TN, 2002, p. 30.
11. Josh Harris, *I Kissed Dating Goodbye,* p. 95.
12. Josh Harris, *Boy Meets Girl,* pp. 181–182.
13. Ibid., p. 183.
14. Harvey Yoder, *God Knows My Size,* TGS International, Berlin, OH, 1999, p. 210.
15. The term "Audience of One" is a concept gleaned from Randy Alcorn, *Safely Home,* Tyndale House Publishers, Inc., Carol Stream, IL, 2001.
16. Randy Alcorn, *Money, Possessions, and Eternity,* Tyndale House Publishers, Inc., Carol Stream, IL, 2003, pp. 94–95.

continued on page 158

continued from page 157

17. Henry Morris, *The Genesis Record*, Baker Book House, Grand Rapids, MI, 1976, p. 590.
18. Randy Alcorn, *The Treasure Principle*, Multnomah Publishers, Inc., Sisters, OR, 2001, p. 28.
19. Henry Morris, *The Genesis Record*, p. 595.
20. Josh Harris, *Sex Is Not the Problem*, p. 35.
21. Ibid., pp. 120, 184.
22. Lisa Bevere, *Kissed the Girls*, p. 146.
23. Josh Harris, *Sex Is Not the Problem*, pp. 23, 47.
24. Josh Harris, *Boy Meets Girl*, pp. 176–179.
25. Ibid., pp. 188–191.
26. Dr. Clifford Wilson, *Visual Highlights of the Bible*, Pacific Christian Ministries, Boronia, Victoria, Australia, 1993, pp. 116–119.
27. Henry Morris, *The Genesis Record*, Baker Book House, Grand Rapids, MI, 1976, p. 535.
28. Several points in this list are taken from *The Gift of Honor* by Gary Smalley and John Trent.
29. *Character Sketches*, Institute in Basic Life Principles, Vol. 1, USA, 1976, p. 273.
30. Gary Smalley and John Trent, *The Gift of Honor*, Pocket Books, New York, 1987, p. 9.
31. Ibid., p. 10.
32. Ibid., pp. 38–39.
33. Josh Harris, *I Kissed Dating Goodbye*, p. 88.
34. This illustration comes from Randy Alcorn, *The Purity Principle*, Multnomah Books, Colorado Springs, CO, 2003, p. 10.
35. Henry Morris, *The Genesis Record*, pp. 583–584.
36. Ibid., p. 642.

CHRISTIAN AID MINISTRIES

Christian Aid Ministries was founded in 1981 as a nonprofit, tax-exempt 501(c)(3) organization. Its primary purpose is to provide a trustworthy and efficient channel for Amish, Mennonite, and other conservative Anabaptist groups and individuals to minister to physical and spiritual needs around the world. This is in response to the command ". . . do good unto all men, especially unto them who are of the household of faith" (Galatians 6:10).

Each year, CAM supporters provide approximately 15 million pounds of food, clothing, medicines, seeds, Bibles, Bible story books, and other Christian literature for needy people. Most of the aid goes to orphans and Christian families. Supporters' funds also help to clean up and rebuild for natural disaster victims, put up Gospel billboards in the U.S., support several church-planting efforts, operate two medical clinics, and provide resources for needy families to make their own living. CAM's main purposes for providing aid are to help and encourage God's people and bring the Gospel to a lost and dying world.

CAM has staff, warehouses, and distribution networks in Romania, Moldova, Ukraine, Haiti, Nicaragua, Liberia, and Israel. Aside from management, supervisory personnel, and bookkeeping operations, volunteers do most of the work at CAM locations. Each year, volunteers at our warehouses, field bases, Disaster Response Services projects, and other locations donate over 200,000 hours of work.

CAM's ultimate purpose is to glorify God and help enlarge His kingdom. ". . . whatsoever ye do, do all to the glory of God" (1 Corinthians 10:31).